The Invisible Tattoo

The Invisible Tattoo

True Stories about Children

Grieving, Living, and Loving after Loss

Edited by Karen Ali and Christina Miskura

Forward by Joseph M. Primo

Morristown and Princeton, New Jersey

ISBN-13: 978-0615914251
Good Grief Publishing

For those who give
to the children of Good Grief

Contents

Acknowledgements

Good Grief is made possible because of people who care. Good Grief exists because society has forgotten how to support its grieving. But, at Good Grief, we remember. The love and support—the community—that is created at Good Grief would not be possible without its dedicated and compassionate volunteers, its loving and passionate staff, committed donors, and all the people that create the Good Grief community.

This anthology was made possible with the leadership of Joe Primo, Good Grief's CEO. Upon the publication of his first book, *What Do We Tell the Children? Talking to Kids About Death and Dying* he wanted to be sure that the voices of Good Grief families were also heard. So, he had the idea to create this anthology. The anthology was carefully edited by Karen Ali and Christina Miskura. Our thanks to Princeton AlumniCorps for providing Karen to this project. Christina was an intern at Good Grief and had a hidden love for grammar. Special thanks to Sandy Bruno, a Good Grief mom and intern, who collected all of these essays and managed this project.

Our friend, Karen Zinn, founder of heart2soul.com, created the cover. And, of course, this anthology would not be possible without the courage of our contributors who willingly shared their story so that others might understand and recognize their invisible tattoo.

Forward

In 2007, I left my job as a hospice Chaplain to join the efforts of a group of people who wanted to provide support to grieving children. As a hospice Chaplain, I witnessed a lot of people die. Many of my patients were young; some were kids. Children often gathered at their mom or dad's bedside at the time of death, just like Tyler did, as he tells us in his essay "Finding My Voice." After the deaths occurred, I often walked the family to the front door and wished them well, knowing that few resources were available to grieving children. So, I joined Good Grief in order to make a difference and prevent children from feeling isolation, despair, and hopelessness as a result of the dysfunction that currently surrounds our society's approach to death.

When Good Grief opened its doors, I could not have imagined what lie ahead. Good Grief's success is because Good Grief is a movement. It is a movement towards creating compassion and understanding, transforming how we support each other when we grieve, educating people about resiliency and what children need after a death occurs, and changing how we think about our living.

I asked the families of Good Grief to tell their stories so others could learn from and get a better understanding of their grief journeys. I explained that this collection of stories and essays would serve as a beneficial resource for families in underserved parts of the country who do not have access to a place like Good

Grief. Similarly, I invited our facilitators – kind and generous volunteers who give a great deal of time to Good Grief – to reflect on their experiences of witnessing someone rebuild their lives after profound grief.

The stories in *The Invisible Tattoo* will change you. Their teachings are both subtle and, at times, direct. Most importantly, the stories are true. As much as society wants us to pretend that death will not come, these stories confront death and remind us about hope, love, and our ability to move forward—not move on or circumvent our pain, but to live through it and come out alive and prepared to live. The day will come when invisible tattoos will be visible, and when it arrives, it will be because the children of Good Grief will have moved us forward and taught us how to grieve and care for one another. That day may come sooner than we expect.

With tremendous thanks to the honesty and vulnerability of its contributors, *The Invisible Tattoo* represents a variety of different experiences. No two people grieve the same way, but when we tell each other our story, we do not grieve alone. This anthology is proof.

Joseph M. Primo

June 2014

Living With Us

*"No healing process will return us to life as we knew it when Santi was with us. That life is forever gone. Santi is not forgotten, though. And he never will be. His voice, his laughter, his beautiful blue eyes, his kindness, his memory, live on **in** us."*

Daniel Abut

My name is Daniel Abut. Together with my wife, Sonia, and our two daughters, Victoria and Caroline, I have participated in the Good Grief program since my 13-year-old son Santiago ("Santi") unexpectedly passed away five years ago of a misdiagnosed health condition.

I want to tell you a little bit about my family's background in the hope that as you read my story, you recognize yourself and your family. I believe we are just an average family, not that different from others. And without worrying you, I want you to understand that the tragedy that impacted our family and turned our lives upside down can happen to anyone.

1

Sonia and I were born and raised in Rosario, Argentina. We met freshman year in college, fell in love immediately, and have been together ever since. Soon after finishing college, we got married. I worked in my family's equity brokerage business; Sonia worked in her family pharmaceuticals wholesale distribution business. Two years later, we moved to Boston so that I could study for an MBA degree at MIT. Sonia studied English first, and then took management courses at Harvard.

After two years in Boston, and upon graduation, we moved to New York. I started my first job in equity research—a career that has spanned three banks over 20 years and continues to date. Sonia started working at the Argentine Mission in the UN. In 1994, our first child, Santi, was born in New York. Sonia quit her job and became a full-time mother. Two years later, our second child, Victoria, was born.

In 1998, we bought a house in Summit, New Jersey. I became a daily commuter to Manhattan. In 2002, our third child, Caroline, was born. I continued working in New York, which involved a fair amount of overseas traveling. The children went to school in Summit, got involved in sports, arts, and a zillion afterschool activities; Sonia became an overqualified chauffeur. Things were going great.

Until one day, one unexpected and fateful day in March 2008 when our almost "picture perfect" lives changed forever. In the early morning of March 12, 2008, I found Santi unresponsive in his bed. We called 9-1-1 and help came right away. Santi was transferred to Overlook Hospital, where he was pronounced dead only a couple of hours later. We were in shock, confused, and baffled. Everything happened so fast.

I still play that horror movie in my head, in slow motion, almost every day. We had no idea what had happened. Later, after the autopsy report, we learned Santi died of a misdiagnosed health condition. It was something treatable, but we did not know he had this condition. By his own admission, the doctor had totally missed it, but that does not bring Santi back.

Without ever voluntarily buying a ticket for this trip, we started our grief journey – a journey that continues to this date and will continue until the day we die. It is difficult to explain with words what we felt, and in many aspects still feel, to those who never experienced grief. As Stephanie Ericsson wrote in *Companion Through Darkness,* "[g]rief is a tidal wave that overtakes you, smashes down upon you with unimaginable force, sweeps you up into its darkness, where you tumble and crash against unidentifiable surfaces, only to be thrown out on an unknown beach, bruised reshaped."

That is how it feels. And, because of that, nobody survives grief unchanged. In a way, you have to start again. It is a new "you" that you need to discover. And you cannot do it alone. You cannot do it without help. Moreover, at the beginning, you do not want any part of this process. You only see emptiness, meaninglessness, and hopelessness all around you. You see no future, no tomorrow. In fact, you do not want a tomorrow. What you want is yesterday, with your lost child in it. And you cannot have it.

On our difficult journey—that has already taken five years—we found two things to be particularly helpful.

First, the ability to talk about Santi and share our story, memories, and grief with others who "get it" because they have experienced similar loss is very helpful. Bereaved parents and siblings yearn to hear the lost child's name because not mentioning him anymore only compounds the tragedy, making you feel that he never existed. Those who have not experienced similar loss may think that not talking about your child may help you to "move on." They are wrong. You do not want to move on. You never move on.

When we try to talk about Santi with people who never experienced similar loss, we often get the unintentionally accusing question: "how many years ago did you say your child died?" as if there is an unwritten statute of limitations on grief. With Good Grief, you get unconditional love and understanding with no expiration date! And that is priceless.

The second thing that has been helpful is to find ways to memorialize Santi to make sure that his legacy and memory live on. Some people do this by writing books, creating scholarships, and planting trees. We have done several things and intend to do more. We built an outdoor classroom at the Summit Middle School, a place that Santi loved. The classroom was dedicated to his memory and carries his name. We partnered with SPARC, an organization that supports the arts at Summit public schools, to sponsor an annual drama workshop for middle school students. Theater was very important to Santi; he dreamed of one day becoming an actor. We have also established the Santiago Abut Foundation, which supports worthy projects such as the renovation of the Summit High School auditorium and an annual college scholarship for a Summit High School senior.

No healing process will return us to life as we knew it when Santi was with us. That life is forever gone. Santi is not forgotten, though. And he never will be. His voice, his laughter, his beautiful blue eyes, his kindness, his memory, live on *in* us. No day passes without thinking about him and we are grateful for his touch upon our lives. We are determined to live the rest of our lives with purpose and to bring Santi with us along for the ride.

Holding Tight

"We feel blessed because we were able to be with him in his final moment. We were able to say our "I love you's," thank him for all he was to us, and hold him tight as he left us."

Loyda Rivera

I guess the only way to start our story is to give you a little background as to how we met. I was 15, he was 16 when we came to be—a cliché, but true. We met in high school, and we became friends, going our separate ways when high school ended.

Ten years later, my family moved to Robert's neighborhood where I got a job on Wall Street about two blocks from where Robert was working. Our friendship quickly renewed. One night, Robert asked me to go for a ride down memory lane. He drove us to our old high school—and the rest is history. We became inseparable. Fifteen months later, we were married. We then shared 20 wonderful years together.

Robert was a big guy, with an even bigger heart, full of love for everyone he met. Besides being a real friend and an amazing husband, Rob's true calling was to be a dad. He adored his babies. Our daughter, Maegan, was the light of his life. Many nights I found him just staring at her and whispering, "I love you." Our son, Tyler, was his mini-me, his shadow, his buddy, and his world. When he was not working, he spent all of his free time focused on being with his children and being the best daddy to them—living a lifetime in every day of his life with them.

Our life was full of special moments, "I love you's," and no regrets. Nothing was ever left unsaid, and for this I am grateful.

Robert passed away suddenly in 2009. As difficult as his loss was, we feel blessed because we were able to be with him in his final moment. We were able to say our "I love you's," thank him for all he was to us, and hold him tight as he left us.

Recovering from losing Robert has been a long, hard road. Without the love and support of our families, friends, and Good Grief, we would have never been able to heal and move forward. Good Grief gave us a safe place to heal by embracing us, understanding our pain, and giving our hearts and souls much needed TLC.

Talk to Your Children

"Even at a young age, Conor was a deep thinker with a sophisticated view of the world around him, often called an "old soul" by those who knew him well. Perhaps that is why he left us so soon. The loss of his humor, intelligence, and kindness leaves a void in the lives of those he left behind."

Jill Scott

Our son Conor was a sweet, handsome, and active high school student. An athlete and an Honors student with a passion for History, he was always interesting to talk with about current events and politics. He played football, ran track, was an expert skier, and enjoyed playing video games and engaging in the occasional Airsoft war with his friends. He was a typical teenager with many friends. When Conor got older, his father took him for ski vacations at different ski areas out West each year. They skied and bonded over steak dinners.

As a child, Conor was happy and active. We spent a lot of time together as a family. We skied, visited museums, played games, and attended almost every one of his sporting events. When Conor was eight, we decided to adopt a baby. By then, he knew that being an only child had distinct advantages and was not happy in the months leading up to the adoption. Then, the momentous day came, and we went to see his new sister. Conor fell in love the moment he saw her and never looked back. As she grew, she called him "Bubby" because she could not say Conor as a baby. She idolized him, and he gave her piggyback rides, teased, and indulged her. Each night, he made a point of visiting her room to say "goodnight." As a middle and later high school athlete, he was never afraid to demonstrate his affection for his baby sister, even at his games. It was a defining and endearing trait to everyone who knew him.

He was a son we were so proud of: confident, caring, and responsible. He was a great role model for his sister and others. When asked what he wanted for his 15th birthday, he asked us to match his $150 so he could raise the $300 needed to sponsor a child to attend Catholic school in Camden. We were blessed. He was a loyal and compassionate friend as well. In their words:

- "His smile will never leave my heart or mind. The word that everyone uses is genuine, he was genuine."
- "You truly are an amazing person. We miss you Conor, and always think about you.♥"
- "I hope that Heaven really does exist and that you're there and that you can watch over me and your friends and your family, and that you can help me

through some things in life because I know that you would if you were still here."

- "You were one of those real friends I had; someone I had deep conversations with. Not very many people can do that. Dude, I miss you so much."

- "We're all having a tough time with this. I just want you to know that I love you man."

- "You left too early. I can't help but cry because someone as amazing and talented as you is gone. One positive thing—God has gained another perfect angel!"

- "I just wanted you to know that he was one of the most genuine people I knew and I try my best to take the attitude he had with me every day. Thank you so much for raising such a loving person."

Even at a young age, Conor was a deep thinker with a sophisticated view of the world around him, often called an "old soul" by those who knew him well. Perhaps that is why he left us so soon. The loss of his humor, intelligence, and kindness leaves a void in the lives of those he left behind.

Conor died by suicide. There were no signs leading up to his decision. By all indications, he was happy, healthy, popular, and responsible. His only risk factor was access to a target-shooting rifle. To all the parents who have healthy, happy, and responsible children, please understand that even the most responsible and stable teenagers can be impulsive. Many times there are signs that lead to a devastating and irreversible decision, but sometimes there are not. No one who knew Conor thought our son could ever do this. Talk to your children regularly and prevent their access to firearms. Our entire community mourns Conor because he was an amazing boy and a beloved friend, but they now recognize if this could happen to us, it could happen to anyone. Please keep your children safe. Conor would want it that way.

When I Trust Their Process

"These children express themselves so honestly, without fear of being ridiculed or misunderstood. Children often comment on how everyone "gets" them and their situation at Good Grief, so they can just be themselves."

Helene Hulse

I first heard about Good Grief several years ago from a friend who had recently become a facilitator. Intrigued, I filed "volunteering at Good Grief" away as something to pursue once my daughters were older. Flash ahead eight years, the last three of which were tormented by my *on/off again* painful separation from my husband. Like fate, in which I believe, I received an email from Good Grief announcing volunteers were needed for their 14th facilitator training class. I applied, without hesitation, believing that the time was right to focus my efforts on helping others rather than dwelling on my pain.

My training class was a cross-section of ages, occupations, and personalities. We were there to achieve a common goal: learning the skills that would enable us to try to understand the grieving process and help those affected by the devastating loss of a family member. With Joseph Primo at the helm, we were taught techniques to improve listening skills, ways to empathize, and methods to help us be compassionate without imposing our views or experiences on those who sought support.

A crucial concept that helped us learn about grief and sadness was sharing our own "Loss Line" with peers. Through this exercise to address our personal losses, we were able to develop a better perspective concerning grief and apply our new skills by listening to each other. I never cried as much as I did that week, particularly in the presence of people I just met. But exposing my pain and talking about it with these compassionate peers established a strong bond of empathy, understanding, and trust. Verbalizing my pain allowed me to face it. Although it was painful and emotional, I said goodbye to my husband of 22 years that day, filed for divorce, and moved on with my life.

Good Grief's mantra, **"trust the process,"** is one I try to adhere to. It provides me with a sense of calmness and contentment. I have gained strength by merely being at Good Grief and through my ongoing experiences there. I obtain wisdom from my co-facilitators and group leaders.

I am fulfilled each week by the time I spend in the Purple Group with my teens—all who lost parents and did not have a chance to say goodbye. These children express themselves so honestly, without fear of being ridiculed or misunderstood. Children often comment on how everyone "gets" them and their situation at Good Grief, so they can just be themselves. They remember their loved one, talk openly about them, or just talk about stuff. Most importantly, they talk about the future, their goals, dreams, and hopes. They are hopeful. That is the most poignant part to me. They do not forget. They do grieve, but they also maintain the courage to move ahead with their lives. They gain strength in sharing their experiences with their peers. They have a bond, a connection, and a home.

It is a powerful thing to *witness,* and I am blessed with this opportunity to step outside my tiny microcosm and see the bigger picture. My two daughters have watched me gain strength, confidence, and purpose, much of which I credit to my experience at Good Grief. In turn, my progress has helped them to get past the turmoil that rocked their world.

At a time when I really needed it, Good Grief has positively affected my life as I have *witnessed* it positively affect others who come here to heal their loss. The trickle-down effect perhaps? Tears of sadness, pride of accomplishment, a gentle stream of healing, an ever-shifting tide of love and loss, hope and healing—Good Grief is an invaluable place, and I am proud to be part of it.

GRIEF

Patricia McKernon Runkle

Grief is a room, invisible.
You are pushed into it.
For a while, it is the only
room in your house.

You stumble around.
No lights. No clocks.
No windows.
Empty.

When darkness is dark enough—
enough!—you cross
the threshold, return
to the visible world.

Dust on your desk,
on the fruit bowl.
Kitchen. Remember to eat.
Living room. Agree to talk.

When dust chafes
your living skin,
you'll step outside.
Sun and wind will be at play

and you'll find yourself smiling.
Really, I mean find yourself—
you've been lost all this time.

You have the whole place back now,
but that room will always be there,
and the door will always be open.

Through the Snow and Sun

"Through the snow and the sun my dad let us know he was okay. This is one of the things that comfort me when I think about my dad's death. The years following his death have not been easy for me, and I have found myself in an emotional turmoil numerous times. Yet, whenever I mention the weather on the day of the funeral or think of the snow and serenity..."

Jean Speckin

My name is Jean. My father, Thomas Speckin, died on November 17, 1996, from colon cancer. My family knew that he was not going to make it, but we were not prepared for how quickly it happened. He was not even sick a full year.

A few days before my father died, he went in for routine surgery to have more of the tumor removed. After the surgery, he slipped into a coma. Since we did not anticipate this outcome, there were no final words.

His most unselfish act occurred later. My mom was going to have to decide whether to leave him in the hospital or bring him home for hospice care. We were going to either go to the hospital each day or see him at home in his bed. Both situations were going to be difficult because the doctors did not expect him to ever come out of the coma.

I like to say that my dad made the decision for us. The day after my mom started thinking about this decision, Dad passed away early that morning. I feel that this was his way of letting us know he did not want to suffer anymore or have my mother, brother, sister, and me watch him suffer either. At that time, it hurt. Now almost 17 years later, I see that this was an act of love so that we did not have to see him that way. We would know that he was at peace and could be in Heaven watching over us.

Being 13 and in denial of his passing, I was unaware of how many lives my father touched. When I look back at my dad's wake and funeral, I see his life was like a story, and the people who came to pay their respects were the chapters. His wake was two days, and each day the receiving line was out the door of the funeral parlor. There were more people than I could count, and I did not even recognize most of them.

The day of his funeral I remember getting ready to walk down the aisle after my dad's casket. For a split second, I picked my head up and looked around at the packed cathedral and thought—*all of these people have gathered here not to mourn, but to celebrate the life of my father.* My dad would not want us to mourn. He would want us to celebrate the life he had and be proud of him. Once I realized this, the tears began to fall silently, and I said a quiet goodbye to my dad. Little did I know that my dad was not ready to say goodbye yet, at least, not at the church.

The funeral mass ended and we began to drive into the cemetery for the graveside service. A light, gentle snow started the moment we drove in. It was peaceful and serene as we gathered at his graveside. The final prayers were said, everyone placed a flower on his grave, and we began to depart from the cemetery. As we pulled out of the cemetery, the snow stopped and the sun came out. That was when I realized my dad had said his final goodbye.

Through the snow and the sun my dad let us know he was okay. This is one of the things that comfort me when I think about my dad's death. The years following his death have not been easy for me, and I have found myself in an emotional turmoil numerous times. Yet, whenever I mention the weather on the day of the funeral or think of the snow and serenity, I recall how my dad chose to say goodbye in the way he felt was most fitting for him. He left us with a feeling of hope, and it is something I will always hold on to.

In my dad's final days, he showed a deep love for his family. Although we may not have been aware of what he was thinking or been able to communicate with him, he showed us that he still wanted to put his family first. He wanted us to know he was okay so that we would not dwell on his death.

I know he is with us now, watching his four grandchildren with great joy. Particularly his grandson, who often has "stories" to tell about conversations he has with Grandpa Tom. I like to believe that he does have these conversations and that there is a special connection between the two.

The Edge

"Battling my own grief for many years led me to helping others with loss. I wish Good Grief had been available when my husband died. Grief is an ongoing process. It is constant work. Serving as a facilitator in my adult group is one of the most important parts of my life."

Meg Glasser

I was never one to "live on the edge." Yet there I stood, trembling, strapped to a gurney at the precipice of a cliff somewhere in a forest in Costa Rica. Clamps and metal pulleys provided my life support and would prevent me from plunging head first into the valley below. "I cannot do it," I started to cry a little and felt foolish. After all, zip-lining had been my idea. I had convinced my family that 30,000 colones was a small price to pay for the breezy feeling of gliding through the jungle like Jane. What could be so bad? A young, strapping Latino guide cheering me on all the way, and, perhaps, the chance to shake paws with friendly howler monkeys on the way down. Somehow, because math is not my strong suit, I miscalculated the height, and now I had a new affinity for the window washers at 1501 Broadway, the New York skyscraper, where I worked after college. Now, here I was, shaking like a eucalyptus leaf. So I did what any sensible coward would do. Without turning my back on my predator, I counted the number of steps to the nearest boulder and sought safety.

Suddenly, my guide who had morphed from Christopher Lambert as Tarzan into "Mr. Snot Pot," my least favorite high school gym teacher, poked me verbally. Having mistaken my fear for cowardice, he assured me that I was not the first tourist to change my mind about jumping and implored me to change my mind again. "Would you do it for a million dollars?" he prompted, but I did not take his bait. Then my 13-year-old son Lukas casually asked, "Would you do it if Daddy was standing at the other end?" "Yes, yes," I replied without hesitation knowing it was a trick question. I lost my husband on 9/11 and no amount of magical thinking was going to make him reappear. Gazillion feet in the air and my loss had found me.

"Pura vida," hissed my guide as if he were a rattlesnake. "Throw caution to the wind." Had my husband done that? Thrown caution to the wind while perhaps leaping out of a window on the 93rd floor of the Trade Center? A brave attempt to save his life? Surely, he would have chosen to jump not for pleasure but for survival. Something fierce awakened deep inside me and would not let go. This jump seemed selfish like it was meant to tempt fate. My loss was staring me in the face now. I stood my ground like a prizefighter and demanded to have my feelings validated without sharing my story. The guide was dismissive. Always my consoler, Lukas scrunched up his knees and sat beside me in solidarity.

The guide then turned his attention on his next victim, my 15-year-old son, Dylan. Like wet laundry on a clothesline, he hung Dylan out to dry on the zip-line. I begged Dylan to reconsider, but it was hopeless. I could have demanded he not go, but I didn't. Carefree and hungry for adventure, he was ready for a challenge. Besides, I held enough fear for the two of us. I packed it on my body like baggage on a luggage cart.

Right before Dylan jumped, I was overwhelmed with fears of "what if?" What if the line broke and Dylan fell? What if his brake did not work and he ran into a tree? After all, this was a tragedy that did not have to happen. Hadn't I brought this on myself? I could have easily said "no" and the worst thing that would have happened—Dylan would have been mad at me for a day. Big whoop, he would still be alive. As a survivor, I was always waiting for the next shoe to drop.

Thankfully, Dylan survived in the end, and so did I. For him, it is wonderful memory, and for me, it was sheer madness.

I share this story because I am a grief facilitator at Good Grief. Battling my own grief for many years led me to want to help others with their feelings of loss. I wish Good Grief had been available when my husband died. Grief is an ongoing process. It is constant work. Serving as a facilitator in my adult group is one of the most important parts of my life. I am in awe of the group—the way they listen to each other and how supportive they are. I understand that people with loss often feel like they are speaking a foreign language. Good Grief is a safe place where everyone speaks the same language and no interpreters are necessary. My group overwhelms me with their willingness to share stories.

As a survivor, I understand the gravity of loss. Just when you think you have got grief beat, it resurfaces. Creating a space for people to talk about loss is so valuable. I feel truly lucky to be involved as a facilitator. These families, whose beauty is unequalled, constantly inspire me. Telling your story often falls on deaf ears, which can be challenging as illustrated by the guide in my story. At Good Grief, people listen!

They Are Not Alone

"Watching them grow, change, and support each other has taught me about the resiliency of children, courage, the power of the human connection and the strength that comes from knowing you are not alone."

Terry Blagdon

In the spring of 2007, while anticipating my last child leaving for college, I started looking for something meaningful to become involved in. After a friend told me about Good Grief, I attended a community workshop called "Conversations on Grief." The workshop was amazing, and I learned so much about grief. I learned that many of our struggles as adults result from unresolved grief and the detrimental effects of failing to grieve. Many people are uncomfortable talking about death; they do not permit themselves or others to experience the grieving process when a loved one dies. I find this interesting because the death of a loved one is something everyone will experience at some point. I discovered that children with a loss are most at risk because they have not yet developed the healthy coping skills necessary to deal with difficult feelings. They do not have enough life experience to know that things will get better. Children who are supported after a loss, however, can heal. They will be better able to communicate their feelings, and ultimately, better equipped to cope with future losses. This workshop confirmed that working with Good Grief would be *meaningful,* and it has truly changed my life.

What happens at Good Grief? Children support each other. As a facilitator, I create a safe space for them to be with their peers, share their stories, and realize that they are not alone. I do not counsel or advise. I simply listen, validate, and allow them to have all of their feelings. It is an incredible privilege to sit, play, and be with families during such a difficult and uncertain time in their lives. Watching them grow, change, and support each other has taught me about the resiliency of children, courage, the power of the human connection and the strength that comes from knowing you are not alone. I know now that when the children come together, tell their stories, show their vulnerability, and experience compassion after the isolation that accompanies grief, they become stronger people.

Good Grief inspires me. While facilitating a group of ten to twelve year olds, I thought I was the one making a difference. However, one night I witnessed a boy tell everyone that he wanted to meet with new participants so he could tell them what happens at Good Grief. He wanted to let them know that, although it is hard, they will be okay. He wanted to give back because Good Grief had helped him so much. This is one of many amazing moments I have **witnessed** that demonstrates the courage of grieving children.

My life has been greatly affected by my experience at Good Grief. I always thought I was a good listener until I took the facilitator training class. I realized that my initial reaction to someone sharing something was to attempt to fix it, provide advice or offer an opinion. It was a challenge to simply *listen*. I understand now how important this skill is and I work on it constantly. My children are happy that I give less unsolicited advice.

I feel privileged and honored to be a part of Good Grief. My life has been greatly enriched these past six years.

The Good in Grief

"Grief is a tricky beast, constantly morphing and camouflaging. It rears its ugly head whenever it sees fit and is not assuaged by logical reasoning or a stern talking to that now is inconvenient. If I learned anything from my own grief experience, it is that once you stop being combative and slowly let it in, surprisingly, it does not consume you."

Corinne Meirowitz

When referring to someone who died of cancer, one often hears the phrase "he/she lost his or her battle." My mother *did not* lose her battle with cancer. She went all three rounds over the course of eight years swinging, fighting, and scraping. Somehow, cancer cheated—played dirty and underhanded. It managed to pin her for three final counts and unfortunately, she did not get back up.

Similar to sports, as a society, we have been conditioned to look for the greater life lesson in "losing." Over the years, I have grappled with the questions: "What was life trying to teach us with this cruel blow? Would anything good come from this loss?" And more importantly, "how the heck does one go about grieving?"

Grief is a tricky beast, constantly morphing and camouflaging. It rears its ugly head whenever it sees fit and is not assuaged by logical reasoning or a stern talking to that now is inconvenient. If I learned anything from my own grief experience, it is that once you stop being combative and slowly let it in, surprisingly, it does not consume you. Grief may trick you into believing nothing will get better or change. Once you start wading through the sludge, however, you begin to cover ground.

Coming to Good Grief was the last piece of my grief puzzle. Since my mother's death, I had participated in traditional therapy and peer support groups. I stared grief down and experienced every emotion in the spectrum. Still, something was missing. I realized that the forums in which I grieved were secretive. Even the peer support group, which was the most cathartic, was conducted with a small sense of shame. "Uh oh, going into Psychological Services on campus, better put my head down and not let anyone recognize me." Learning about Good Grief's mission coincided with what I have always believed: grief is universal and should be out in the open in our community. We tend to isolate ourselves in our grief when it could ultimately serve as one of the most powerful connections between us all.

I have been privileged to **witness** how these children are changing each other's worlds without fully realizing it. The kids forge ahead and throw large life questions out: "Why did my parent die? What would I change if I could go back in time? What am I taking away from this death and life-altering experience?" In a short time, a special environment was created in which one participant noted simply "we trust you and each other."

Every time children attend a *Night of Support*, they are accomplishing something impressive—something most adults struggle with. They are opening their hearts, stepping outside boundaries, and taking a huge risk by being authentic and vulnerable. It is beautiful to watch them go from heavy grief work to light moments of simply being a child. At school, they may be labeled as "that kid whose parent died," but at Good Grief, they are just kids. Their joy is infectious and a reminder that life goes on and still holds wonder and hope.

Knowing the bitterness of death can make our own lives sweeter, if we so choose. Although these families have suffered great losses, they are already on the road towards great gains. I **witness** them slowly begin to find their "good" in Good Grief. The journey may not be linear and picture perfect, but that is okay, because there is finally a place for families to go and simply be.

My Perfectly Awesome Sister

'I wanted to curl up in a shell like a turtle and hide for the rest of my life. Harsh reality slapped me in the face and forced me to continue on as if everything was peachy keen. It was not, and I kept shutting myself out from everyone and everything—friends, family, dance, and school."

Rebecca Russell

Kate was awesome—not perfect. Although, I cannot help thinking she was the epitome of perfection. She was captain of her varsity softball team, loved coconut, Coca-Cola slurpees, and was a health freak. She wanted to be famous like J.K. Rowling and have her name known throughout the world. Notice how I am using the past tense? Well, she passed away in her sophomore year of college with an incomplete future and bright smile disappearing all at once. And this is where I get angry—angry at how she was taken when she had so much potential to offer the world. Why am I here when I barely have an idea of who I am? Sometimes I think I should have left instead because she could change the world, whereas I am stuck under my bed sheets dreading the inevitable morning routine. It just is not fair.

Kate passed away during a stupid spring vacation to stupid Punta Cana, Dominican Republic. There really was no explanation as to how; she was gone. When it was confirmed, all my mom received was a lousy telephone call from God knows who saying "Kate's dead." That is it. Done. Finished. One lousy telephone call and my world crumbled under my feet. I fell so hard. I was only a naïve twelve-year-old brat without a care in the world at the time. Seriously, I was a despicable human being and appreciated nothing—not even my eldest sister.

Now I think if I had taken the time to learn those sweet little nothings of Kate's—her favorite color, animal, T.V. show, and more—maybe this would be a bit easier. At least I would feel as if I was closer to her. But I feel so far apart, and it hurts like hell. All of those trips to 7-Eleven, random movie nights, and mornings with her flopping onto my Disney Princess clad bed trying to wake me were all taken for granted. That is my biggest regret.

When I first heard about her death, I was really numb and shocked. I really do not recall what I was feeling at the time, but I have settled on "feeling nothing"—at least until the night of the funeral. That is when it really sunk in and I had my first major breakdown. I have cried before, but you know those uncontrollable sobs that seem to go on forever and you cannot stop them? Well, it was that kind of crying. I was in my bathroom, which adjoined my parents' room. Luckily, I am a silent crier so no one heard me, and that is exactly how I wanted it. I felt the need to be strong for everyone else: Mom, Dad, my sister Megan, uncles, aunts, and cousins. There really is no reason I can give for this attitude, but there it is. Take it or leave it.

So then came the whole "get back to normal" phase, which irks me to even type because nothing will be normal ever again (but, whatever). I had to return to school someday, and the time came way too soon. I think it was a day or two after we found out. By then, word had spread, and basically everyone knew. Ugh, it was awful. I did not make it through the whole day. Instead, I called and asked my uncle to pick me up after sixth period. Eyes seemed to burn a hole in the back of my head and every sympathetic look got my blood boiling. I cannot explain why this bothered me because teachers and students were only trying to be nice and help. The thing is that they did not understand that I just wanted to be alone. I wanted to curl up in a shell like a turtle and hide for the rest of my life. Harsh reality slapped me in the face and forced me to continue on as if everything was peachy keen. It was not, and I kept shutting myself out from everyone and everything—friends, family, dance, and school. I felt so lonely, and it was my fault. For the rest of sixth grade, I was mostly mute. And probably seventh grade too for some time. I was always the "shy Russell," so there you go.

Slowly, very slowly, I started to get "better." Better being a rather languid word to use, but I cannot find another that fits. Anyway, I stand here now as a relatively shy, relatively crazy (to those who know me) sophomore in high school. An optimistic girl with wise, blue eyes that look beyond what others want to see. I learned a lot the past four years, but it is not all gumdrops and rainbows. Right now I am confused and not really sure who I am or what to do with myself. I suppose that is normal, but I cannot help thinking that I am trying to be like Kate. I drink tea and play softball like her and my sister Megan. When I first started softball, I thought I was only seeking activities that I can do, something fun or spontaneous. Now, I am wondering if perhaps I am trying to impress Kate, her former coach, Megan, and those who are watching. I want to be good enough for them. More importantly, I want to make Kate proud.

Today, I appreciate everything and try to say, "I love you" to my family as often as I can (as cliché as this may sound). That is the funny thing because you see—I am a better person now. It kind of hurts to say this because I cannot help thinking it was a good thing, in that sense, that Kate passed away. I immediately shake that thought from my mind whenever it pops up like a jack in the box. Wow, it gives me shudders to think that, but I have to be honest. Not that I want Kate to be gone, but I know she can see how I have changed and how I feel—I don't know—more worthy of her. More worthy to be her sister. I only wish that I had known that four years ago.

Me, Myself, and Matthew

"Even with all of the amazing support, I was still worried. I did not want any of this to screw up Matthew's life! I knew that I would not be able to undo how I handled John's death or what I said to Matthew, and I knew that this would either help or hurt him."

Cindy Clark

Welcome to our story. We were just regular people. My husband, John Kelly Clark, was the friend that everyone wished for. He was fun, loyal, and made you feel special. He was a simple man, a salt-of-the-earth kind of guy who absolutely loved being a husband and father.

In the winter of 2008, John had a toothache. We learned that it was from a cancerous tumor, and he underwent eight months of treatment. John passed away in January 2009, a few months before our son, Matthew's, fifth birthday. During John's illness, Matthew was very involved with his dad's care. We talked openly about what was happening to Daddy's body and about death and dying.

Throughout John's diagnosis, I was the one to talk with Matthew about what was happening to his dad. John and I would discuss everything beforehand, but I took on the role of the messenger. I did the research, scoured websites, and talked with doctors, pediatricians, and hospital social workers. After going to the experts, we developed three simple rules that have since guided all of my conversations and decisions for Matthew: Be honest; Keep it short and simple; Repeat reassurances over and over again.

I reached out to a friend who facilitated at Good Grief, and I was able to practice how I would talk to Matthew. I spent a lot of time planning and worrying about this, but I was lucky in that each time I had a serious conversation with Matthew, he made it easy for me. He sometimes would not say much and just want to play; other times he would ask questions or remain quiet and tearful. He was very much aware of what was happening in our family, but he continued to be a little boy and do little boy things. It was very difficult for me to fight my intense urge to "protect" him, but I have learned that the truth is always better than what he could conjure up in his mind. I believed that Matthew deserved to have the opportunity to grieve the loss of his father just the same way as the adults in his life could.

It is overwhelming when someone dies. I had to organize the services, handle finances, be a good mother, and still take care of myself. My emotions were constantly swirling, and I was not sleeping much at all. I was fortunate to have full-time help in the house as my parents moved in with us for several months. I learned to say "yes" to those who offered help. Family and friends delivered meals, walked the dog, and gave Matthew rides to practices and play-dates. I informed everyone how I was handling communications with Matthew, and I requested that they let me know if he brought up his dad in conversation. I surrounded Matthew and myself with people I knew would support my wishes and his well-being.

Even with all of the amazing support, I was still worried. I did not want any of this to screw up Matthew's life! I knew that I would not be able to undo how I handled John's death or what I said to Matthew, and I knew that this would either help or hurt him. Books and websites were helpful, but as time went by, I felt that we needed something more personal. So, I turned to Good Grief.

Experts tell you that young children express themselves through play and arts and crafts. If Matthew and I were to do these same activities at home, the experience would be too solitary. Dealing with John's death would remain just between the two of us. Good Grief allows Matthew to be in a place with other kids who are going through the same thing that he is. He loves going to GoodGrief, and it has given us a sense of belonging and community.

By all accounts, Matthew is a normal and healthy little boy with amazing coping skills. He is funny, has a lot of friends, and remains active by playing sports. His teachers describe him as happy, compassionate, and kind to his classmates. What more could a mother want for her child!

I truly feel that the one thing I got "right" was to introduce Matthew to his peer support group at Good Grief. Being a part of this organization has made a tremendous difference in our lives. I realized that it is not time that heals—it is what you *do* with the time that heals. Good Grief has helped us develop ways to keep John part of our lives and in our hearts and minds in a healthy, productive way. For us, Good Grief is not always about the grief—it is about ways of living with the death in our family.

I Am Willing Not to Know

"I have learned so much from listening to these teens. They have taught me courage, how to put one foot in front of the other, and that life goes on without the person who has died. They have shown me that they find a way to continue to honor themselves while honoring the one who has died."

Shelley Miller

I have had the good fortune of volunteering in many different ways, and I have always felt that working with children would be the most rewarding. During my volunteer search three years ago, my cousin told me about Good Grief. I decided to take the facilitator training, and my thought processes changed while being provided with insight, laughter, tears, friendships, and the challenge of silence. I learned these five small, yet life-changing, words: Be willing not to know.

My first year as a facilitator found me in a roomful of 3-6 year olds. They gazed back at me, wounded yet joyful, childlike, but now coping with intense feelings of loss. No longer naïve, these amazing children were part of a group who now had to understand why their parent died. They had to learn a new way to navigate through life.

While sitting with the children on my second night of facilitating, I found myself in the middle of four of "my kids" who were in the midst of creating dream catchers. They asked each other questions about how their parent had died and shared honest answers in a matter-of-fact way. "How did your mom die?" "My dad's death was more horrible than yours!" "Oh yeah, well my dad died of cancer, and it was worse than your dad!" "How could you not know how your mom died?"

The children guided their own conversation. They were taking care of themselves in such an adult-like manner. While silently stunned by the "grown-up" nature of their talk, I felt privileged to sit with these precious children. They were sharing what they needed to share, and they were in a safe space to do so. I had many questions that I wanted to ask the children, but I just listened. I was willing not to know.

I have now been facilitating with the teen group for the last two years. I have learned so much from listening to these teens. They have taught me courage, how to put one foot in front of the other, and that life goes on without the person who has died. They have shown me that they find a way to continue to honor themselves while honoring the one who has died. We have explored questions of religion, war, death, hurricanes, homework, music, sports, and violence – very real subjects in a very real and scary world. Yet this is all done while the teens mourn the loss of their parent. The teens share each other's happiness and understand each other's sadness. I feel privileged that they trust me while sharing their feelings, joys, accomplishments, and questions. While I have questions too, I remain willing not to know.

These children have shown me a path in life that I would never have known. They have taught me that it is possible to share laughter while grieving. They have shown me how to be present in life, and they have taught me that one learns more through listening than by asking questions. They have demonstrated the definition of resilience. They have shown me the essence of trust.

I am forever grateful and truly humbled to share this experience with each and every one of the teens who have entered my group. I am hopeful that by bearing *witness* to their stories that "my" teens will always be free to share their loss with others as they continue to grow. I have faith that they will continue to honor their parent. I hope that these teens will feel the courage to go on to do good things with their lives, and I hope that their participation at Good Grief allows them to continue their journey in a meaningful way. Above all, I hope that they, too, will be able to listen and be willing not to know.

Trust the Process

"Many years ago, I lost my father to brain cancer, leaving my mother with two young children, a teenager and me (21). I learned firsthand how my father's death devastated our family and changed our lives forever."

Kate Rutherford

About six years ago, a friend invited me to a fundraiser for Good Grief. At the time, I did not have any idea what Good Grief was about or how it would change my life. The fundraiser lasted an hour, and I heard heartbreaking stories from children who lost a family member through death and from volunteers who supported them every other week. Everything I heard during that hour hit home for me. Many years ago, I lost my father to brain cancer, leaving my mother with two young children, a teenager and me (21). I learned firsthand how my father's death devastated our family and changed our lives forever.

I then knew I wanted to become a facilitator. I participated in the facilitator training six months after I attended the fundraiser. The training was one of the most eye-opening experiences of my life; it changed how I viewed the world and my family. By the end of the training, I could not believe how different I felt and the bond I had formed with the ten members of this group.

A couple of weeks later, I walked into my first *Night of Support* with the young teen group. I was very nervous since I did not know what to expect. I did not want to mess up and do something wrong. At first, the participants did not talk much, so we introduced age-appropriate games to break the ice. Not only did they begin talking, but they quickly formed a bond. The conversations ranged from school to friends to the temptations all around them. They realized that they could talk about anything at Good Grief. It remains confidential, and they are not judged.

After two years, I added an additional *Night of Support* to facilitate the 6 to 9 year olds—a group with a lot of energy and so much to say. They love their Good Grief home with its rooms for activities, music, and games. Often, I hear the children say that Good Grief is their favorite place. It is hard to fit everything they want to do into one night. The most challenging part of facilitating this age group is trying to get them to speak one at a time because they have such a strong desire to share.

As a facilitator, I have some very memorable moments that stand out. In my young teen group, I had a participant who attended Good Grief for over four years. He rarely spoke about the death of his loved one. When I first met him, he seemed angry and sullen. He often stated that he only came to Good Grief because he was forced to do so. On several occasions, he was disruptive and we had to speak to him about his behavior. He also mentioned that he had no interest in school.

By the time he was a junior in high school, he talked about his aspirations and attending college. I will never forget how proud he was when he told us he had been accepted by his first choice. When he turned 18, he drove himself to Good Grief. He became the leader of the group and was very welcoming to new participants.

There are many rituals at Good Grief. One such ritual is attending an "opening circle" with all participants at the beginning of the evening. Another is attending the "closing circle" at the end of the night. Until his last night, this teen never participated in either ritual. He did everything on his own terms.

On his last night, the teen stood in the closing circle, and I joined him. When a family leaves Good Grief, facilitators are invited to join the group in closing circle. This is a wonderful closing ritual for families so they know that their time spent at Good Grief will not be forgotten. I cannot tell you how proud I was to be standing next to this young man on his last night. I wished him good luck at school. He turned to me and said, "Thank you for everything." **Trust the process.** When I think about this young man and his journey at Good Grief, I know that I will never again judge whether a participant is getting anything out of the process. People grieve in different ways.

Good Grief has changed my life in many ways. I think the most important is that I have become a better listener. I feel honored and privileged to be in the presence of these families every week.

Wedding Days Widow

"I never imaged the dead could actually speak!"

Sheila Grifo Fredericks

My husband Glenn died in September 2009. His niece, whose wedding day was set for May 2010, visited him while he was home under hospice care. They knew it would be the last time they spoke to each other. He told her that he was very sorry he would miss her wedding. They said their goodbyes.

The wedding date arrived, and I dreaded the thought of going. I did not want to go without Glenn nor did I want to dress up three young kids for the wedding.

In my nervousness about going to the wedding, we arrived early. We went into the place, and no one was around. So, we sat in the lobby. Suddenly, a telephone started ringing, and a voice over a loud speaker blared, "Glenn, pick up the phone. Glenn!!! Pick up the phone. GLENN IN THE KITCHEN—WILL YOU PICK UP THE

PHONE?" I looked at my daughter and remarked how strange that the person's name was Glenn.

As I told the story to a few arriving relatives, I realized Glenn had no intention of missing this wedding. Glenn was a fan of the Three Stooges; his initials are GF, and Great Falls is what I called this wedding because so many people fell down. In fact, a film clip from the wedding went viral on the Internet, showing one of the bridesmaids crashing down to the floor after being introduced. It was very much in the stooge style! Could Glenn have actually been tripping these people? He was such a clown!

Several months later, in October, my nephew got married. This was a little easier to get ready for, but I was still missing Glenn. During the ceremony, they had a moment of silence for those who had passed.

I passed a table with his picture on it, but I managed to hold it together and had a good time. On the ride home, however, I was upset. My sister had driven, and I told her that I expected a sign particularly since there was a picture of him and a moment of silence. I just expected some confirmation that he was there, too. We were traveling fast on the parkway when I said it.

No sooner had the words left my lips before we had to abruptly slow down. I looked in the distance to see a car jutting out across the lanes. I clearly saw on the license plate "GF." The cars shuffled around slowly as we came to a full stop. Somehow, the car that was in the distance ended up in front of us. I could not believe my eyes! The license plate read "UGF-59C." Glenn's initials were GF, his birth year was '59, and leftover were the letters "UC?" I was so astonished I had to take a picture. I never imagined the dead could actually speak! Another sister left the wedding ten minutes later driving the same route. They did not hit any traffic.

What Will I Do?

"The loss of a child is not so easily shared, even between parents."

Denise Smyth

My name is Denise Smyth. My husband, Phil, and I have two children, Philip and Natalie, the great loves of our lives. On February 23, 2012, we discovered that Philip, who turned 21 the month before, had died. It was sudden and unexpected. I was devastated, heartbroken, and terrified. This does not really describe how it felt—it is merely the best I manage right now.

A year later, I would love to report that I have said "yes" to the universe and agreed to soldier on. Maybe I have, maybe I am. Perhaps, I believe if that is true, I should feel differently than I do. Better, more peaceful. I am told that it is a process, a progression. God save us from "processes" and "progressions."

But, it is like this. Walking around the early Sunday quiet of Whole Foods with its gorgeously arranged produce. It is the peppers that take my breath—the God-given red, yellow and orange. Not the green ones, their waxy dullness is unappetizing. Clenched against despair amidst all that abundance, I ask "what for?" I mean, what the hell? I see Philip looking at me wearing the black leather jacket I gave him, the one I am wearing now which makes me look like a biker-chick. I see him—my beautiful boy, in his navy blue suit, laid out in a coffin.

My son in a coffin. In what universe does life make sense?

I want to tell my story: what I was doing when I found out. How long I sat on the landing where Phil told me they found him. How long it took me to understand what he was saying. What I said when I stopped screaming because, try as I might, I could not scream this away.

And I want to know Phil's story. But I do not want to ask him; he does not need to relive it. I do not think he trusts reliving it. "What for?" I think he would say. He works to find his peace, building his world, brick by brick. I think that is what men do. Me, I spent a year sitting in the rubble, ashes in my hair, moaning when I was not wailing. Phil tries not to go to the dark place. I am there enough for both of us—three when you count Natalie.

Maybe I can talk to Phil about it one day. Maybe he will fill in the gaps of what I cannot remember and give me his version. When he is ready. It seems important, although it cannot really matter. If we disagree about the events, do we get a do-over? Would I be able to figure out how I could have stopped this, changed this, given us the happily-ever-after that required nothing other than our two children living longer than we do?

I want details. All I have of my son is my story, and sorrowful as it might be, I want it all. I want to know exactly how Phil felt when he found out. Shock, disbelief, and grief—obviously, I know this. But I want to know how he experienced it and where he felt it in his body. Because if he tells me how he felt, maybe I will not be so alone. Perhaps he can help me locate the words I need to find my way home. I do not know any other way. I have faith in words. I believe that if I can say it the way I need to, I will be well. I believe that what haunts me are the stories I do not yet know how to tell.

The loss of a child is not so easily shared, even between parents. Phil and I went to a parents' bereavement group a few months after Philip died. I am not unused to support group. Years of AA taught me that when a problem seems bigger than you are, finding people who have dealt with such problems might help. Not so this time. At least with alcoholism, the path to healing has some sort of shape—if you are a drunk and you want to start living, you have to stop drinking.

But how am I to find my way on this path? In AA, we talked about drinking vodka and wine, the stupid and dangerous things we did, how we almost died from embarrassment, and how we almost died. We talked about what we felt like. We identified. And in our sameness lay our hope and help.

What was I supposed to identify with here? Maybe I am a mother and you are a mother. I lost a son and you lost a son, but you did not lose Philip; you did not lose my son. Your "identification" was not what I wanted. It changed nothing. Besides, you could not possibly understand. For you to understand I have to be able to explain what I felt like and I could not. I could not say it to anyone because I did not have the words. I could say "grief" and "despair" and "desperation" but that was not what I really meant. Those were ordinary words, words I had used before. Losing Philip was nothing like anything before. I would have to invent a language to tell you. And this loss of language unmoored me: I was slipping, slipping away, gone to a place where I could see and hear you, but you did not make any sense.

One year later, I am in a new version of surreal. I have stopped telling everyone, including the cashiers where I shop and the telemarketers who breach the do-not-call barrier, what happened. I shower regularly. I change my clothes daily. I even put on makeup again. But my heart is broken; a chunk of me is gone. I wake up every day wondering, "what now?" I feel kind of crazy to be functioning like a normal person when I am anything but. I am small and too scared, and I want my son. Sometimes I wonder who is the parent because I cry to Philip "help me, please help me. Please come home, please do not be gone. I miss you and love you, and what am I going to do without you, Philip?"

Our New Normal

"We have a new normal now. We have an understanding of what it feels like to have someone taken from you way too early. My children have a sensitivity that many others twice their age do not have."

Sally Kelly

It is hard to believe that my husband, John, died over two and a half years ago. Looking back, I can say that was definitely the longest day of my life. I was working, it was a beautiful sunny day, and my morning routine went as expected. Suddenly, he was dead.

What was I going to tell our children? More importantly, how was I going to tell them? Would I be able to answer their questions? I was so dazed. I could not believe this actually had happened.

My friend went with me to pick up my children from school that day. I kept trying to figure out what to say. I had no idea. None. That was the longest two-mile drive of my life. My children kept firing questions at me. I remember telling them we were having a family meeting; however, my friend is not part of our family.

As we all walked into our home, they immediately sensed something was wrong. My oldest child (10) asked me, "What happened? Where was Dad? Why was everyone at our house except Dad? Tell me," he said.

I sat them down and said, "Dad died this morning." I just blurted it out. It was awful—beyond awful. Their cries, their shrill screams, the confusion had started. How could I explain that all of a sudden he was just gone? There was no explanation, no "goodbye," no understanding of why.

Over the next couple of days, we went back and forth to the funeral home. We slept together in my bed. We cried and held each other tight. It was so surreal, so unbelievable. Our home was a revolving door of family, friends, food, and well-wishers. I do not even recall most of that week. It was just the beginning of what we would face.

Saturday was the first night of the wake, and I knew it was not going to be easy. I went to the funeral home early with my children. It was just the four of us. We were going to spend time alone as a family saying goodbye to John.

I saw my first open casket at the wake for John's father 14 years earlier. I was 30 at the time. And here my young children had to see their father in a casket at the ages of 6, 9, and 10.

During the wake, I had terrible chest pains. I was sure the pain and anxiety I was experiencing was normal. I was positive it was due to stress. As the evening went on and my pain got worse, my brother insisted that I go to the hospital. The short version is I was having a heart attack. I spent the next six days in the hospital.

My children went through two more funeral home visits, the funeral, repast, and burial alone. They had to bury their father without their mother. I had difficulty processing what had happened and could not imagine how they were going to do it.

The night I was discharged from the hospital I was supposed to attend a Good Grief event my cousin invited me to a month earlier. I was not able to attend that night, but, that was the start of Good Grief for me.

Since John's death, so many things have happened in our lives. The children have grown so much. They miss him every day, and we talk and laugh about him all the time. This is all in part due to Good Grief and what they have given us. My children say the children at Good Grief understand. They have a special bond that ties them together. It is a sisterhood/brotherhood. Good Grief feels good.

We have a new *normal* now. We have an understanding of what it feels like to have someone taken from you way too early. My children have a sensitivity that many others twice their age do not have. They know what deep sorrow feels like, but they have learned how to deal with such sorrow. They have learned how to be compassionate, how to sit in a room and be comfortable in silence.

They have worked to be happy again. Although they have felt tremendous pain through their Good Grief friendships, they are able to laugh and be children. They are okay. We are **okay**.

If Only There Were A Quick Fix

"Life is fragile. This is not the typical lesson for young people. Most people face serious grief at middle age, and it's a huge struggle. When tragedy hits a young person, it can cause a crisis in faith and hope that only time, support and love can heal."

Sally Calcagni Muscarella

Our grief counselor continues to remind us that, "the bigger the love, the bigger the loss." Our loss of Leni, my beloved husband and father of our girls, Annie and Nicole (at the time, 21 and 16), was enormous.

Leni was a "bigger than life" personality. Leni did not miss a party. He made the party. He loved life. He loved his girls, his family, friends, sports (all sports and especially the Green Bay Packers, LA Dodgers, tennis and golf), food (Italian of course) and drink (Dewar's), journalism, music, the Internet company he built, political debates (he represented the far left), coaching, community service, Boston College, Morristown, St. Peter's, Morris County Golf Club, and Vermont. His friends and family formed a long line that stretched a block to attend his wake. The turnout was a testament to a good man and deep friendships.

Annie (a college junior who had just ran the Boston Marathon) and Nicole (a high school sophomore who was about to become student body VP) were supposed to be immersed in the best days of their lives. Leni died suddenly, without warning, after cardiac arrest, a seven-day coma, no brain waves, and the horrible decision to remove life support.

Life is fragile. This is not the typical lesson for young people. Most people face serious grief at middle age, and it's a huge struggle. When tragedy hits a young person, it can cause a crisis in faith and hope that only time, support and love can heal. There are no words that can ease the pain, though kind and loving words and actions throughout the grieving process are essential.

In the minutes after Leni died, we resolved ourselves to follow in his example: *WWLD—what would Leni do?* Annie knew that Leni loved our church, family, and helping others. He also understood the importance of the kitchen to family life. She had a brilliant idea to direct memorial donations to a kitchen fund at our church. In two years, with the proceeds from the memorial fund, we built a new, beautiful soup and parish kitchen.

Several weeks after Leni died, Annie and Nicole immersed themselves in summer jobs working with kids. They enjoyed the children and doing work that was fulfilling but not mentally exhausting. Annie had given up an internship to return home. We felt a need to help each other and be together.

During that first year, we were in survival mode. We did only what had to be done. We left town for holidays to change the scene. Friends and family surprised us with random—often anonymous— acts of kindness, visits, meals, and TLC. It was not necessary to say anything. Their presence and their steadfast love made a big difference.

It was vitally important for Nicole to be in the presence of other teens at Good Grief going through the same experience (Annie was away at college and unable to participate). One of my vivid memories of Good Grief's adult meetings was seeing the pain on the face of widows and widowers two and three years after the death of their spouse. Their "years-old" pain was no less than my "months-old" pain, although I expected otherwise. It takes so long to process a tragedy and to re-form your life and family.

Leni's absence was difficult for everyone. Although it was difficult, we muddled through together—keeping some family traditions, like the annual summer picnic for 50+ relatives, and forming new ones. Despite the challenge of caring for my mother who was suffering with late stage Alzheimer's, the geographic separation of our family, and the temptation for us to want to occasionally crawl under a rock and hide from family gatherings, we maintained our close family ties.

While living in the aftermath of loss, daily routines are a struggle. Life changes—new jobs, new schools, new challenges, and new relationships—are fraught with peril. There are constant ups and downs. Care and concern from true empathetic people (rather than those who unload problems or want to wave a magic wand) make a difference. Professional help is essential. We have been blessed with great family and friends.

Based on the experiences that Annie, Nicole, and I shared, it appears several different phases of healing from loss (with varying lengths, emotions, and outcomes for each of us) exist.

The first phase is grief and survival. It lasts for a year . . . or maybe two or three. It feels totally draining and devastating. Our very dear friends who know loss call it "the lost year" because you remember so little. Your school and work productivity are severely impaired.

The next phase is gradual acceptance. It can last at least a year . . . or two or three. It feels even worse than the survival phase at times as you struggle to release the old reality. This phase is a battle with yourself to slowly let go of the part of the past that you no longer have. It's characterized by internal thoughts—"I can't," "I don't want to," "it's no fun," "it will never get better"—until you surrender.

The last phase is rebuilding: a long period that includes trying new things and discovering what brings happiness. Three and a half years have passed since Leni's death. There is greater acceptance and increasing hope. This year, on Leni's birthday,

Nikki celebrated his birthday by sharing her hysterically, funny card for him.

There are no quick fixes. I am hopeful that the sad times that Annie and Nicole endured while young will enable them to live their lives in a purposeful way, appreciating the gift of life and relationships. Hopefully, their dad will serve as their role model, and they will have his courage, strength, and zest for life. I would like them to find partners who embody his character, drive, personality, and love. Living life to the fullest despite the hole in our hearts is not only the best path, but also a great tribute to Leni, a wonderful father and husband.

Grieving is Healing

"Having grown up with loss, I am keenly aware of how difficult it is for most people to deal with someone who is grieving: not knowing what to say or do and often just avoiding the person altogether."

Jonathan Asher

My journey begins as a four-year-old boy whose father died suddenly of a heart attack in 1962. I was the last one to see him alive.

"He was never sick a day in his life," relatives used to say. And that frustrated me. Perhaps if he had been sick, they could have found a cure, and he would still be alive. But worse than that was, "Well, now you're the man of the house." Really? You think that is a good thing? For a four-year-old (or any age—I heard it all my life and hated it), it is not a great honor. It is a tremendous burden and scary as hell!

Of course, I did have to be "the man" at 14 when my mother died and I had to choose her casket at the funeral home. It was an unusual but necessary task for someone so young; I certainly felt much older than 14.

I also hated being thought of differently or given special consideration because my father had died. That sort of backhanded compliment: "Well he's very smart, considering he has no father" really annoyed me. I would rather have been judged on an even playing field, and then everyone would have known just how smart I was.

In fairness, I did have it *differently* and had to grow up quickly in some ways. It was very tough dealing with the absence of my parents' loving guidance throughout my life and not having the ability to make choices based on the greatest of possibilities versus being limited by circumstances.

It was also difficult dealing with important life events. I remember a scene in the movie *An Officer and a Gentleman* that I suspect few others recall. It was immediately after the cadets graduated and several cadets were standing with their families. For just a split second, Richard Gere's character is standing alone looking around. He looked pained, at least, I thought he did. I felt his pain because I have also been alone in special moments when family surrounds everyone else.

Fortunately, I have memories—my own and others that were shared—and photographs and keepsakes of my parents which I cherish. I also have an old black and white silent film, but I have no sense of my father's voice. I have mentioned the importance of these things to the adult group I facilitate at Good Grief to make them more mindful of keeping them for their children.

When I learned of Good Grief, quite by accident, while searching for non-profit groups that could benefit from *pro bono* design services, it immediately clicked that I should be part of this organization. I knew I could relate to the children who had experienced loss, and hopefully, they could benefit from my experiences.

I have learned so much from my experiences as a facilitator, including a new respect for all that my mother endured after my father died. As I observe my adult group face various challenges with courage, strength, and perseverance, while keeping their children's well-being paramount, I am awed and inspired. It reminds me that my mother faced similar circumstances when I was a young boy.

Having grown up with loss, I am keenly aware of how difficult it is for most people to deal with someone who is grieving: not knowing what to say or do and often just avoiding the person altogether. Since joining Good Grief, I have become painfully aware of the pervasiveness of this problem. People not only avoid dealing with the grief-stricken, but some say things which they believe are helpful but are terribly misguided—"Well, don't you think you should be over it by now?" And whether "by now" is one month, six months or six years, the answer is "NO, I'll never be over it." Hopefully, in time, with love and support, I will find a way to live with the pain and lead a more normal life. There is no magic timeline for grief. It takes as long as it takes!

My hope is that with an organization such as Good Grief in the world, people will develop a greater understanding of how to be supportive to those who are grieving. Everyone will be comfortable just being with the person and understanding that "being is doing."

They will not offer "should and should not's" (grieving people do not need a lot of advice), and they will stop acting as if grief is contagious.

I have experienced many wonderful moments as a facilitator. These moments have given me inspiration and have allowed me to offer words to nudge someone forward on their journey.

Recently, I received a card from a member who had *closed*, thanking me for being caring and supportive. She thanked me for sharing my story about my father's death because that was the moment when she realized her son was going to be okay—that one could survive loss at such a young age. And with that, she was able to move forward.

Knowing that my story could have that effect and help this wonderful family deal with their loss and heal through their grieving helped me feel that my journey has been worth it. Pay it forward, indeed!

What Brings Me Back

"Being part of Good Grief has reminded me that change comes with loss. I have learned from the children and adults how to live with change and loss in ways I had not thought possible."

Ellen Pierson

What keeps me coming back as a facilitator for Good Grief? I volunteer on two *Nights of Support*; one for children and one for adults. This volunteer "work" is the most important thing I do, because it is meaningful on a personal and professional level.

On a personal level, I was 20 when my mother died; my brother was 15. I was away at college and I have the indelible memory of hearing my father's words telling me about her death on the telephone. Equally unforgettable are the memories of how my brother struggled to process the death of his deeply loved mother after her brave four-year struggle with cancer.

On a professional level, as a former psychotherapist in private practice, I know that the most painful journeys for children and adults are grief journeys. I also know that when family members are included in that journey it helps with the client's growth.

But why is Good Grief's model of witnessing others' pain and growth so powerful? It is because the facilitators, children, and parents are not alone. Feeling acutely alone is what most of us feel along the route to adjusting to our loss.

The facilitators help me come back. Our peer support, understanding, and awareness of what the children and their parents are enduring makes these volunteers treasured friends. It is the parents and children, however, who really pull me into the fold. I look forward to seeing them every week with as much unconditional acceptance as I can manage to help them face issues that arise in their chaotic lives.

Recently, I noticed a girl who appeared numb, tense, and unable to express herself. One night, she curled in a ball with her fist slowly pounding the floor and her face hidden. Eventually, she responded to her peer group, playing, joining in an activity and even smiling. When I witnessed this special girl having some "normal" time with others like her at Good Grief—that was joy.

The new *normal* that the children and adults experience each day of their new lives without their loved one is a process of wonder, fear, disorientation, and discovering new paths in familiar situations (with friends, extended families, at school, and in their neighborhoods). When the familiar situations are strange because the beacon (the lost parent, sibling, or child) is no longer available, the child or adult's peers provide light simply by sharing that they also feel lost and in the dark about how to live now that the loved one is no longer present. Coping with grief, accepting it, and creatively finding outlets for grief happens in the activities and discussions.

Being part of Good Grief has reminded me that change comes with loss. I have learned from the children and adults how to live with change and loss in ways I had not thought possible. I see and hear children and adults finding new ways to live their lives, which inspires me in living with my retirement and aging issues. There is no going back! It is right now that matters and living as fully in the present as possible is how to get through change, how to get through loss.

Still Keeping Up

"He was the first one to climb on the roof to clean the gutters, sunbathe, or help take down a bee's nest. He was fearless. Our family was filled with excitement and wonder with him."

Judi Cianciotto

He had a huge, perfect smile that could melt anyone's heart. Even if you were mad at him, you had to forgive him or even laugh when he flashed that smile. Nicholas was a strong-willed fifteen year old who never accepted the word "no." Not because he did not want to listen, but because he always had a valid reason why he was right. He was determined.

He lived to be with his friends and to do the next thing. He loved dirt biking, snowboarding, construction, and fishing. Tragically, his love of fishing is how he died. He could not wait for ice fishing season to start. He began planning with friends. On Sunday, the day before the accident, he had me drive him to several stores to get gear. As we shopped, I told him how thick the ice had to be and that it made me nervous. He said I was being silly; he knew where it was deep and he would be careful.

That day, the lake was filled with ice fishermen and wind iceboats. He was so excited and could not wait to get out there. The next day after school he and his friend fell through the ice and could not be saved.

Two weeks after he passed, we went to see a famous medium not knowing if we would be chosen for a reading but knowing Nicholas's strong will and determination. Of course, he came through with details only he knew. He assured us that he was okay. He was always concerned about his family's welfare, and he did not want us to worry. He explained the accident through the medium. He wanted us to know that he did not disobey us—it was just an accident.

We acknowledge signs that we believe are from him. When his song, Don't You Worry Child, comes on at the perfect time, his dad finds a dime or his mom a penny, a cloud in the sky clearly spells, "hi" or a strong wind blows, we thank him.

He loved attention and did not like to be alone. When his friends were not around, he clung to his two younger brothers to the point of being annoying. Although, you knew deep inside they loved the attention too. He wrestled them until exhaustion. He snuggled with his little brother, hugged and squeezed him, and called him his little snuggle bug. He did the same with his girlfriend and when they broke up, he was left with a heavy heart.

He looked and acted like a tough guy, wearing diamond earrings, Levi skinny jeans, and flannel shirts. His family and close friends knew the real Nicholas was caring, sensitive, and loving. He loved to make people laugh, even at inappropriate times, like in church or school. After he died, we were told that he once started a popcorn fight in a movie theater on a class trip. While cleaning out his backpack after his passing, I came across a detention note for bringing a snowball into the school lunchroom. That was Nicholas.

Life with Nicholas was not always easy, but it was filled with love and passion. Sometimes it was exhausting to keep up with him. He had a fiery temper that we did not understand and was diagnosed with ADHD in the 9th grade. Once we understood what he was dealing with, we knew how to handle situations better. He matured a lot in the last year of his life, and we could see the motivated, talented man he was becoming.

He loved construction and worked with his father, who had the same passion. Together, they built beautiful things. He was his father's best friend. He loved to help people and took great pride in doing so. He practiced baseball with his younger brother and wanted to teach him to dirt bike in the worst way. He assembled his little brother's dirt bike Christmas morning. Sadly, he died two weeks later and never saw him ride.

He was also close to his other brother, who was 16 months younger. They fished together and had "deep" teenager talks, which only they knew about. He was my shopping companion and tagged along to make sure I bought the "good" food. He made a list of "Nick's favorite foods" and taped it inside the kitchen cabinet. We will keep the list forever.

He was the first one to climb on the roof to clean the gutters, sunbathe, or help take down a bee's nest. He was fearless. Our family was filled with excitement and wonder with him.

Now we live a careful, more planned life, afraid that something might happen to one of us. His death crushed not only our immediate family but also his grandparents, aunts, uncles, cousins, and friends. We have a strong, loving family on both sides, and we thank God for that. It is with the help of our family, friends, church, and Good Grief that we are able to heal and try to live the new, different life that has been handed to us.

Our faith in believing that we will be reunited with Nicholas in Heaven helps, although it does not make missing him any easier. The kindness and love we have received from perfect strangers amazes us and gives us hope for healing. We will rebuild our family, and the feeling of being destroyed will be replaced with beautiful memories of a wild, exciting life with Nicholas. Nicholas would always end his "goodbye" to us with a huge smile and the words, "I love you" and that is how he will always be remembered.

Bubba

"The next morning would be the hardest single event that I would have to face—telling my girls, then seven and eight, that their father was dead. No words would be harder to say. I still do not know where I found the strength."

Sandy Bruno

Our story began in 1996. I was working in a flower shop when a big, strong man walked in with tears in his eyes. He was there to make floral arrangements for the services of his younger brother. He caught my attention, and I soon came to know this sensitive man as Marc—my future husband.

We dated and then married two and a half years later. Our family became complete after the birth of our second daughter in 2002. But our happiness did not last when Marc had a massive heart attack later that year. He survived and was doing well, and we flourished as a whole family for the coming years.

Marc had many nicknames. The girls affectionately called him Big Guy, but I knew him as Bubba. He was my guy—the man I had waited for all of my adult life. He was my very, very best friend, the man who loved me for who I was and respected me like my father did. We certainly had gone through enough with Marc's heart attack in our short marriage—we were good, right?

As I woke in the middle of the night in March of 2009, I knew that the answer to my previous question would not be answered the way I had dreamed. Nine paramedics asked me questions as they worked on the man I loved so dearly. As I looked into Marc's eyes, I could see him saying, "goodbye" to me. That would be the last time I would see those loving eyes that made me feel so whole each time he looked at me. He would be pronounced brain dead approximately fifteen hours later, and his organs were retrieved for donation later that night.

While those were the most devastating hours that I have ever endured, I knew that the worst was still to come. I had left my girls at home with my family, and they would be fast asleep when I returned home from the hospital. They had gone to bed one last time being the daughters of a loving dad who was attentive and always there for them. The next morning would be the hardest single event that I would have to face—telling my girls, then seven and eight, that their father was dead. No words would be harder to say. I still do not know where I found the strength.

As the months passed and the girls and I went back to school, we muddled through our lives without a dad and husband. The girls' elementary school pointed us in the direction of Good Grief, an organization with peer support groups for kids who had lost a parent or sibling. I believed that this was the way I was going to help the children and myself. I knew how to be a good parent, but I needed help living with my own grief and helping my children get through theirs. We never felt alone at Good Grief. We were supported with our grief and loss. My girls were taught healthy coping skills and found comfort in knowing that they were not alone. I found friendship and acknowledgement in my own circle of adults.

A few months before Marc passed away, we were standing in the kitchen together after I had a hard day. I looked at him and said, "I just want someone to take care of me." He responded, "that is not my job—that was the job of your mother." Marc made me see that I had to take care of myself. Deep down, I truly believe that he knew he was not going to be around to watch us grow old together. His words stay with me every day as I attempt to raise our family and do what is best for our girls.

Marc made me a better person. He was my better half, and he taught me how to love completely and cherish important moments. He taught me that things could get better no matter how bad they seem to me. He gave me the gift of hope. Above all, he gave me the greatest gift I have ever been given—our girls. I hope he would be proud.

I have a newfound strength and hope for my girls and myself since Marc's passing. I have discovered that my passion and commitment is helping children, and I have focused my education in social work. I have decided to give back to the community and recently completed Good Grief's facilitator training. I am a member of the organization's Family Advisory Board, and I also completed Good Grief's internship program for my Associate's degree. I could think of no better place to get involved than this wonderful organization—one that has so profoundly changed the lives of my family.

Not only does Good Grief support children and families through their grief journey, but I believe that it also teaches lifelong listening and coping skills. I listen to these children help one another through difficult feelings that would leave any adult speechless. They support and nurture one another when the outside world has expected them to "get over" their loss. Good Grief is a refuge for these children as they forge ahead with their lives while still grieving and missing that special someone.

Marc passed away four years ago, and we still miss him each and every day. Our lives are forever changed. Although he is gone, we do not love him any less. Because of Good Grief, we have learned to live and cope with our loss. This support system and community has also changed our lives forever—but for the better.

Catbus: My Love Song for Noah

"Noah will always be my child of silliness, creativity, laughter, and unfathomable resilience. I feel such gratitude to those who cradled our family through an experience that could not have been anticipated. There is no preparation for what we have suffered."

Anne Harris

I often think about the way that our son, Noah, experienced every little detail of life with exponential joy and appreciation. Each little card that played music, each special balloon or trinket, would elicit so much delight. Noah had huge gratitude for little kindnesses.

And Noah's positive outlook, from infancy to age six, went even further. He always astonished me when he heard stories or watched movies with both positive and negative features; he noticed *only* the good. Even watching *Star Wars*, Noah saw Darth Vader and observed, "He might seem bad, but he wants to be good!" He saw the best in everything and everyone. One of the best, most unanticipated treasures of being his mom was not only seeing the world through his eyes, but having it filtered in such a beautifully, optimistic way. Noah's world was overflowing with hope. That was my Noah: luminous, sunny, uplifting. So, in his short but brilliant six years, Noah grew up contented and deeply loved. And he beamed love in return.

Early on, Noah discovered cozy, adorable costumes. When he was small and not yet sick, he often dressed as a plush little frog, or let me put him in a soft blue rabbit suit that made him look like a perfect stuffed animal at Easter. In time, these fun and fuzzy creatures would come to characterize Noah for all of us, including the doctors and nurses. When we walked through the clinic door, they grinned at seeing a frog, bunny, duck, cow, elephant, tiger, dragon, mouse, Dalmatian, giraffe, dinosaur, bumblebee, lion, Wild Thing, Optimus Prime, Teenage Mutant Ninja Turtle, Dash, Darth Vader, Spiderman, Luke Skywalker or Obi Wan Kenobi. These costumes became far more than superficial coverings; they became identities and, I believe, crucial comforts for Noah.

It was a couple of years later that we experienced an even more magical era of costume transformations. Our family became entranced with Hayao Miyazaki's films *Howl's Moving Castle*, *Spirited Away*, and *My Neighbor Totoro*, and associated costumes soon emerged. Noah's original Totoro costume, painstakingly made by friends, was followed by Totoro's sidekick Catbus. Nothing elicited a more awestruck and delighted response in Noah than these costumes. With the Catbus costume, Noah put it on and would only take it off for washing with the most intense coaxing. At those times, he stood longingly in front of the washer and dryer and waited. Then, with joy, he would pull the costume from the dryer and say, "Mommy! It's ready! And it's still warm!"

I have often stepped back and tried to figure out, "how was it for Noah, inside those costumes?" Physically, I know they felt soft and cozy and safe, but I also believe they evoked delight in people, which fueled Noah's spirit. The costumes must have also given Noah a liberating sense of transformation. Noah found his own power to change at any given time. I am so proud of him for discovering that—for embracing new identities and creating his own extraordinary world. Because as magical as it was for him, it was even more magical for the rest of us. Beyond magical.

Noah will always be my child of silliness, creativity, laughter, and unfathomable resilience. I feel such gratitude to those who cradled our family through an experience that could not have been anticipated. There is no preparation for what we have suffered. But the good I have seen in others, the generosity and vastness of love—that must be recognized as a silver lining, a lesson in the goodness of people and the productive, rescuing energy that comes from such generosity and compassion. Such love helped raise Noah above the circumstances we faced. That love helped him live as a happy child who enjoyed life, played robustly and lived fearlessly, packing an amazing lifetime into six precious years.

I recall people telling me—even from the *moment* that he was born—that Noah was an "old soul." That he had "deep and understanding eyes." That he came here to teach us something or to teach me something. That he wants me to make sense of *this* incalculable tragedy, of his loss. I continue to grapple with what it means to have had such a wondrous child come into my life, only to leave again so very soon.

Noah taught me that adversity is highly subjective. Noah rarely thought of himself as sick. He just accepted the medical environment as a part of his ongoing life. He took control and worked out his own methods for when and how to take medicine. He asked for particular nurses on particular days to suit his mood. His buddy from Duke, the site of his first transplant, even called him "Little Napoleon" at age two because Noah loved to command 6-foot-tall Jeff (who referred to himself as Noah's walking jungle gym).

Noah gave a lot to other people, too. He shared his joyful, silly, and fun spirit with those around him. But he also gave tangibly in the world. Because of Noah's struggle, at least 100 new people joined the National Bone Marrow Registry. Countless blood donation units have been given on his behalf. Numerous units of umbilical cord blood were banked or donated for possible transplant use because of Noah's story. Thousands of dollars have been donated in Noah's honor to organizations that conduct cancer research, provide medical treatment, or assist children and families impacted by the disease.

Noah only lived a few years, but he had a huge impact. He is forever a soul of love and ringing laughter in my heart. One of the things I cherish the most is Noah's beautiful voice. What Noah said every day, particularly during the last couple of years, demonstrates the gift that we were all able to give him. I will tell you those words that he said often and generously. And I beg you to think about their meaning—the way they tell us how Noah saw all of us and experienced the world. Here is what he would say. Every day, and many times a day, most often spontaneously:

"I love you too."

My Sister Threw A Banana

"At Good Grief, talking is an act of bravery, and listening is the greatest gesture of love there is."

Libby Doyne

"My little sister threw a banana at my head this morning." Everyone laughs. "A banana. At my head. For no reason." More laughter. His face loosens.

"I was so mad. I really wanted to hit her. But I didn't want my mom to get upset. So I just sat there and didn't do anything. But can you believe that?"

He looks around the room. "I guess it is kind of funny, now that I think about it."

The room goes quiet. Everyone starts to look around at each other. We hear a rubber band snapping inside someone's mouth. Braces. The mood is light at the moment, though it is not always.

At Good Grief, talking is an act of bravery, and listening is the greatest gesture of love there is. Sometimes we laugh, sometimes we cry, sometimes we scream and yell. But mostly, we are honest. We walk into the room, we shut the door, we light a candle, and we get to be honest. However lovely or ugly our truth, we get to tell it. And for once, the heads in the room are nodding up and down instead of side to side. For a few hours, no one will tell us what we should or should not feel, what needs to be kept to ourselves, what is too painful to hear. No one will cut us off or shut us down because of their grief, impatience, exhaustion, or frustration.

What happens at Good Grief is not magical. It is hard work. It is missing sports practices and play rehearsals; it is driving long distances and feeling the burden of another event for which we need to be on time. And most difficult of all is having to face thoughts and feelings that we spend most of our time hiding, stifling, and pushing away. Those horrible thoughts that pop into our heads that we cannot unthink: *"Who will walk me down the aisle? What will I do on Father's Day? Was this my fault?"*

As a facilitator, I do not have any of the answers, and I cannot tell them what to do or how to feel better. The only gift I can offer is my presence: my full attention, without distraction, judgment, or authority. I am simply there to witness and to facilitate their process. What comes out of their mouths ranges from beautiful to heartbreaking to profound to hilarious. It is raw and unrehearsed and jumps casually back and forth between ordinary and extraordinary.

Sometimes I am surprised that the room surrounding us is strong enough to hold these children and all that they are going through. If those four purple walls could feel the force of their crushing grief, earnest love, and sincere effort, the decorations would surely fall off the walls, the light bulbs would burst, and the small wooden table would crash through the floor. But the room does not feel their pain; it never budges. Despite how grief sometimes makes us feel, the planet keeps spinning and gravity continues to hold us safely to the Earth. And we have no choice but to go on.

And they do. With laughter and joy and anecdotes about bananas. At Good Grief, they have found a small, still space where they can sit with their peers and share things that they cannot say to anyone else. They can have their individual needs met while helping to meet the needs of other children who are just like them. Their grief is seen, heard, and acknowledged. And they need this more than anything else. Because they cannot possibly cry in math class every day. Because their friends are fed up. Because the rest of their family is also grieving. Because no one understands. They are tired, scared, and overwhelmed, but they still have to catch their 7:20 a.m. bus, ace their science test, learn the notes to that song, and make that big tackle. They do not get to hide under the blankets and come out when they feel they are ready. Their persistence is heroic.

I truly consider having found Good Grief to be among the greatest gifts I have ever received. I am eternally thankful for these children, for their bravery, and their trust. I am honored to be a *witness* to their beautiful lives. I am proud every time they show up. And I am beyond grateful to share their room.

Enough Support to Handle a Mountain Man

"There is no correct way to grieve or correct way to feel. This is how the Good Grief program "changed" my life. Good Grief let me know that I did not have to feel guilty for not constantly thinking of Stevie or feeling sad, but if I did, that was okay too."

Adam Natoli

I was not sure what to expect when I began my training to become a facilitator at Good Grief. One might expect to meet others with psychological, counseling, or educational backgrounds that are looking for experience or a way to use their education, but this was not the case.

A dozen people sat inside a small room that barely held the circle in which we were sitting. The group consisted of three generations of people. Although there were vast differences in our backgrounds and ages, I soon noticed similarities regarding why we were there. Everyone mentioned a sense of being "called" to Good Grief. Almost one third of the group had gone through the process of losing someone themselves. There was a passion in their voices; it was clear that Good Grief had changed their lives. I looked forward to letting Good Grief change my life too.

Three and a half months later, my life did change. One of my best friends was placed on life support and expected to die. Stevie is like a brother to me, a part of my family. We have been friends for ten years, since the beginning of high school. We spent our summers fishing together almost every day. I was told that Stevie would be taken off of life support on Friday, the day after I visited him in hospice. The doctors estimated that he would die shortly after its removal.

I decided to go fishing on Friday. I could not think of another way to feel close to Stevie. I grabbed my gear and drove to "Stevie's Spot." I fished all day, smiling and laughing. I talked and joked around with Stevie as if he was standing next to me, and although he was not, he was. After Stevie and I finished fishing, we always skipped one stone apiece. That day I skipped two, the first for me and the second for Stevie. Of course, the second stone skipped twice as many times; Stevie was always better at skipping stones than I was. It was not until I started walking back to my car that I started to cry.

During the days following hearing that Stevie was going to die, I experienced a tidal wave of emotions. There were times, like while fishing, when I would think about Stevie and start laughing. How could I laugh? How could I not be constantly devastated over what happened to one of my best friends? The answer: because everyone grieves in his or her own unique way. There is no *correct* way to grieve or *correct* way to feel. This is how the Good Grief program "changed" my life. Good Grief let me know that I did not have to feel guilty for not constantly thinking of Stevie or feeling sad, but if I did, that was okay too.

I was told that my experience with Good Grief would change my life, but that is not entirely true. In the same way Good Grief facilitators offer support and do not change how people feel, my experience as a facilitator also provided support and not change.

The Same Different Life

"When thinking about how our lives have changed since David died, it is surreal. It's even odd writing this story, knowing he is not here to edit my work. Life is the same but different without David. We try to keep him present in all that we do. We talk about him, tell stories, remind each other of his funny sayings and what he loved; we try to keep him with us."

Heather Mark

How do you capture a person in 1,000 words or less? David would have no problem doing this. He was an amazing writer. A journalist by trade, he was the managing editor for a real estate newsletter. David broke stories about the credit bubble, sales of iconic buildings, and the fall of investment portfolios. In his private life, he loved to write about affairs of state and had a blog during what he considered the *dark days* of political journalism. David wrote two novels but was never published. That was his big project for the year he died. He was going to make final edits to his book and submit it again to agents. There are so many sayings about how life has other plans for us—in this case that is so true.

We both thought there would be more time. David had beaten leukemia nine years earlier; he was "cured." We were told that you do not get leukemia after you are cured. He did. He was going to be okay, though. The doctors assured us that the treatments had advanced since his first battle. His sister was almost a perfect match . . . everything would be fine. Two months after he was diagnosed with this deadly disease a second time, he died from a cerebral hemorrhage. His platelet counts were too low to operate, so the children and I had to say our last goodbyes to the best man I have ever met.

David was brilliant, kind, and loving. He adored his family and friends. He was passionate about life and having fun. He instilled that passion into our children. David was an optimist with a wicked sense of humor. He loved underdogs—he was a Red Sox and Cubs fan from childhood. Before the Sox won the World Series in 2004, he used to say "The Sox and the Cubs would be tied going into the final game of the Series with a tied score in the bottom of the 9th and the world would end." He would explain the world would have to end since neither of his teams could win. He would always laugh when telling this tale to people. He loved to laugh; it was a hearty, infectious laugh. His sense of humor was what made me fall in love with him in the first place.

Because David was a writer, he had a way with words. His favorite expression was, "It's just as easy to make an excuse to do something as it is to not do it." He was the first to say, "why not?" instead of "why?" He loved to create and sing silly songs for the children. His song titles ranged from *"He's a Bear"* to *"Put Your Tongue in Your Mouth."*

When thinking about how our lives have changed since David died, it is surreal. It's even odd writing this story, knowing he is not here to edit my work. Life is the same but different without David. We try to keep him present in all that we do. We talk about him, tell stories, remind each other of his funny sayings and what he loved; we try to keep him with us. We do this by keeping our traditions and adding to them so that we can make the most of our lives. I know David is with us, keeping us safe and helping us though challenging times.

There is nothing people can say that makes it better or worse. It is not fair or right that you have lost the love of your life, the man with whom you were going to grow old, and the man who was "the everything" to your children.

But I know what David would want for our children and me. It is to stay strong and make every day count. To find the good in a bad situation and keep him present and alive in our hearts. Most of all to enjoy our lives. That is the best way we can honor and remember him.

I'm Sorry, You Have Cancer

"Surely you don't become a widow at the age of 33 only to find out you have breast cancer at the age of 34. Unfortunately, my reasoning was faulty. I had breast cancer! What was I going to do?"

Desiree Polakowski

"I'm sorry, you have cancer." These are the words that I heard on that seemingly ordinary Monday morning. It had already been an unimaginable year.

On December 5, 2010, I woke up to find my husband dead. He was only 38 years old. The amount of trauma that I experienced on that fateful day is incomprehensible. My primal instinct was to prevent the children from seeing him and then call 9-1-1. I then worked furiously to try and resuscitate him, but there was no response. When the medics arrived, I hoped and prayed that they would somehow bring him back to me. They had to! He was the love of my life, the father of my two beautiful children! And then the news—"I'm sorry ma'am, we couldn't save him." Every plan we had for our future vanished in an instant. Or so I thought.

The days, weeks, and months that followed were filled with pain. The agony I felt was devastating, but worse was the inability to heal my children's suffering. I had to somehow get a four- and seven-year-old to understand that their dad was never coming back. Although it was agonizing at times, what I learned surprised me: kids are incredibly resilient. With the help of Good Grief, I was given the tools I needed to keep the lines of communication open. I allowed my children to freely express how they were feeling, and we gave their dad a presence in our lives. I would reassure them by stating, "I bet Dad is smiling right now, watching you hit that triple" or "I know Dad is so proud of how well you are doing in school."

In the beginning, they showed some resistance to being so open, but therapy really helped. Good Grief was particularly beneficial because it gave them an opportunity to connect with other children who experienced similar loss. Now, when another child asks one of my children, "You don't have a dad?" they say with complete confidence, "Of course I do. Mine's just in heaven." The first time I heard these words uttered, my heart filled with pride. In that moment, I realized that my children were well-equipped to deal with whatever life may bring their way. And with that realization came a deeper understanding of my life's purpose.

I wanted to be in a profession that would help children realize their full potential, particularly those dealing with adversity, but how?

At the time of my husband's death, he was the sole provider. I was unemployed. He did not have life insurance. I had completed my B.A. in Psychology and always planned to return to school once the children both reached school age. I realized if I was going to support my family, my plan had to be revised immediately.

Three months after my husband's death, I applied to Fairleigh Dickinson University's M.A./Certification program in School Psychology. One month later, I was accepted into the program and began my studies in the fall of 2011. I was the only "mature" adult among a group of recent college graduates. At first, it was intimidating; however, I rose to the challenge and discovered that I was able to achieve tremendous academic success. Managing the demands of full-time graduate school and being a single mother was trying at times, but I made it work. The pride and sense of accomplishment I felt those first few months was empowering; everything seemed to be falling into place when another fateful day came.

It was Thanksgiving weekend 2011, and we were emotionally preparing for the one-year anniversary of my husband's death. I was lying in bed when I came across a lump in my breast. I immediately showed it to my mom, and we both agreed it was nothing. Being a single mother, however, I knew that I could not take a chance.

On Monday morning, I strolled into my doctor's office with my Statistics textbooks in hand. I had an exam the next day and was concerned with how this might interfere with my studies. I believed that the appointment would definitely have a positive outcome. I thought, "Surely you don't become a widow at the age of 33 only to find out you have breast cancer at the age of 34." Unfortunately, my reasoning was faulty. I had breast cancer! What was I going to do? My children had lost one parent already, and they could not possibly lose another! The fear that seized me that day quickly lifted. What was left behind is the person I am today. Just like my children, I am resilient, and well-equipped to deal with whatever life brings.

It has not always been easy. I have had my share of struggles, but I continue to persevere. Sixteen months later, I am still battling. What was preliminarily thought to be early stage breast cancer turned out to be Stage 4 metastatic disease. Every three weeks, I have to go for treatment. My future is unknown. Then again, so is everyone's. This is a lesson, unfortunately, that I know too well.

I choose to focus on the positive: my children are thriving and my condition is considered stable, which allows me to pursue my goal of becoming a school psychologist. In fact, two years have passed since I was first accepted into the program, and I plan to complete my externship during the next academic year. The doctors tell me there is no cure, but I refuse to accept that. It is not denial – it is maintaining a positive outlook. I believe that if the doctors can keep me alive for ten years, there will be a cure. In the meantime, I plan on doing everything in my power to ensure I remain strong, healthy, and an active member of society. It is my hope to leave my mark on this earth for whatever time remains. I do not want any special praise for having dealt with my adversities in a positive way. Rather, I hope my will and determination will serve as a model for generations to come because I plan on using my life experiences to assist me with counseling the youth I will be privileged to serve. Undoubtedly, I will meet children in my career that reach a point in their lives where they think, "I can't go on," but I am here to tell them, "Yes you can, and you will!"

My Father's Death Saved My Life

"We must embrace pain and burn it as fuel for our journey."
- Kenji Miyazawa

Kelly Higgins

The memories of my father will never leave my heart. Although I did not have a chance to say my official "goodbye," I was fortunate to be by his side during his final days. The three simple words "I love you" that we exchanged every day are all I need.

My father's death saved my life. It opened my eyes to what is truly important in life: love, trust, maintaining solid relationships, listening to others, and never taking anyone or anything for granted.

Two months after my father died, I quit my job—a job that I thought I would be stuck with my entire life and dreaded waking up to every morning. I am glad that I finally had the courage to leave. I now work for a great firm with wonderful, caring bosses. I work without stress; I know that they appreciate the work that I do every day.

My relationship with my mother has grown enormously during this time. Before my father's death, we were at each other's throats almost every day. His death brought us closer because we needed the other's support; it gave us a chance for a relationship. If we had not shared this loss, I am not sure where we would be now. Instead, this experience has made me realize how fortunate I am to have such an amazing woman as my mother.

I left an unhealthy on/off relationship that I had been in for six years. I had finally gained the courage to walk away and not look back. I am now in a healthy, loving, committed relationship with a man who puts a smile on my face every day. We are building a wonderful life together. He supports and helps me with every step I take towards achieving my goals. I am truly thankful for him and our life together.

Then came yoga! After many sleepless nights, nightmares, anxiety and panic attacks, my counselor and a friend suggested that I try yoga. My first yoga practice changed my life. When I step on my mat or into the studio to practice, a sense of peace and calmness flows throughout my body. I have never experienced anything like it. So much so that I am in the process of obtaining my yoga certification (200 hours!) so I can share this gift with others. I want to teach people how to de-stress and provide them with an opportunity to find peace. I am looking forward to my journey teaching others about the amazing benefits of yoga.

I have also learned that is okay to ask for help during your grieving period. My help came from Good Grief, an organization that helps children and teenagers deal with the grief of losing a parent or sibling. The connections I made through this organization will last a lifetime. It has been a huge part of my healing process. My facilitator helped me through the most difficult time in my life, and I am grateful to her to this day. Do not try to do this alone. Whatever you do, do not hide or run from your grief and pain. Please know that you are not the only one out there feeling this pain.

Realistically, we all have bad days where we are overwhelmed with grief, anger, sadness, and regret. Do not fight these days; let them happen, we all need to feel this frustration to appreciate the rest of our amazing days. My amazing days are filled with passion now. I have dreams and goals, short and long. I started to read and write again, passions that I always loved but lost throughout the years. I spend my time doing what I love on the weekends with my three unbelievable best friends: my loving boyfriend and our two pups. I have amazing, solid, friendships that will last forever. I surround myself with my amazing family including my two beautiful nieces and nephews who always put a smile on my face.

My father's death saved my life. I am still healing daily, but everyone heals differently and at a different pace. Take your grief and pain and turn it into something good and use it to motivate you to be a better person! My life today would not be what it is if I had not gone through the experience of losing my father. My father played a role in every step I have made these last two years and continues to do so daily. He is always by my side.

One Telephone Call on 9/11

"I wish I could say that I felt sad initially, but I did not feel it right away. It is kind of like when you get a cut. It is so sharp that you do not feel the pain. It is not until you see blood that you know you are hurt. I sensed something was different, but I did not know what it was and whether it was bad."

Dylan Glasser

They say, "What doesn't kill you makes you stronger," but I disagree. I think that what doesn't kill you, doesn't kill you. Nothing could have prepared me for the event that would change my life forever. Everything came to a crashing halt on the morning of 9/11. While I was only four-and-a-half years old when my mother received "The" phone call, I remember everything. My own experience with loss is what brought me to Good Grief as a volunteer.

I was a well-behaved kid by all standards. I did not fight with my brother. I ate my vegetables. I did not watch a lot of TV, and I slept in my own room. But I did have a flaw. I was messy. I painted the walls, the floor, and the kitchen table. My babysitter, Wilma, let me do this so I was thrilled when she arrived that Tuesday morning bringing paint, brushes, and poster board. We prepared to paint at the kitchen table while my mother made her grocery list. Peanut butter was on the top of the list. My brother and I painted for a bit, but we really preferred dipping our brushes in the dirty paint water and flinging it at each other. We splashed dirty water everywhere, but Wilma never yelled at us. She even let us finger paint while eating goldfish crackers, which really was not easy to do. The telephone rang. My dad was calling my mom from work. He was in Tower Two of the World Trade Center.

We continued to make a mess and play. At this point, I was not concerned. My dad always called when he got to work. Sometimes, I even got to talk to him. I liked that, because he always left before I woke up in the morning. My mother took the telephone to the den. My dad wanted her to turn on the T.V., but, she was unable to locate the remote control. I often moved it while I was setting up my Thomas the Tank Engine toys and building tracks. She accused me of hiding it somewhere, but even though she located it, she became frantic. She watched the TV intently. Suddenly, the telephone began ringing off the hook. She asked if Wilma could get us out of the house for a while. Later, I learned she did not want us to see what was happening on the TV.

Wilma raced to pack up Goldfish and Juicy Juice. She could not get us out of the house fast enough. At that point, I knew something bad had happened, but I did not know what. Wilma told my mother that she was taking my brother and me to the park. When we left, my mother was in the den crying. I was not terribly concerned; I was excited to go the park because it had a wooden train where you could hide in the boxcars. Wilma put us in the double jog stroller that my dad used when he competed with us in the Turkey Trot Race on weekends. We headed out.

For the rest of the day, we played in the park until it got dark. If something bad was going on, Wilma did a good job hiding it from us. She helped us down the slide and pretended to chase us through the obstacle course. Eventually, we finished playing and headed to the train station next to the park. I was happy because I loved the train station. It was where Dad took me to watch the trains. We would sit on the cement stairs overlooking the platform, and my dad would announce the arrival of each train in the voice of a Thomas the Tank engine character. On those magical afternoons, my dad turned the Summit train station into the Island of Sodor. We liked Percy and Gordon, but we did not like Cranky the Crane, because the wooden one I had at home did not have a magnet strong enough to lift the other trains, and it always broke. Dad and I watched the "Choo Choos" for hours until it was time to go home for dinner. I am told "choo choo" was my first word. On that day, Wilma took us to the train station to wait for my dad to get off the train, but of course he did not. Besides, he had driven to work that morning. If he was coming home, he would drive up the driveway like he always did, and we would wait for him on the front stairs. He would flash his lights and honk loudly so we would know he had arrived.

We headed home because Wilma was sure my dad would be there by now. When we arrived, his car was not parked in the driveway. Instead, I saw a party going on at my house. A crowd of people waited in the kitchen to surprise my dad. I recognized Aunt Heidi, Uncle Randy, who worked in the same building as Dad, Grandpa Herbie, Grandma Barbie, Uncle Billy, and Grandpa Gerry. Some neighbors also came to celebrate, along with a few of Dad's work friends. Everyone was waiting for Dad to come home. I was stunned by the lack of balloons, cake, and presents. While everyone partied, Mom made telephone calls, trying to figure out what time Dad would get home. I do not recall where I slept that night or if I even went to bed. My babysitter may have taken me home with her, or I might have slept at my grandparents' house.

It would be days, weeks, months, and even years until Mom accepted that Dad was one of the victims killed in the Trade Center attacks. She was convinced he was lying in a hospital with amnesia and, at some point, would remember who he was and come home. She held onto hope as long as she could.

As the weeks passed, my uncle drove her to New York where she travelled to hospitals, telephoned morgues, and waited on lines at emergency centers, looking for Dad's name on the lists of "identified" dead. I never went with her. Instead, I stayed with my grandparents, and Mom would call to see how we were doing. She did not want to disappoint us by returning home without Dad.

Months later, when other victims' families received bone fragments of their loved ones, the only thing we got was my father's charred ID that he carried in his wallet. That is when my mom finally agreed to hold a memorial service. Her best friend, Cesca, flew in from San Jose, California and she helped Mom plan a musical tribute to Dad. Friends and family gathered at the Reeve's Reed Arboretum where they listened to Mom's clients sing Dad's favorite songs. I did not go. Instead, I spent the day at Wilma's house, playing with her nieces and nephews.

I wish I could say that I felt sad initially, but I did not feel it right away. It is kind of like when you get a cut. It is so sharp that you do not feel the pain. It is not until you see blood that you know you are hurt. I sensed something was different, but I did not know what it was and whether it was bad. I liked all of the attention I received. I was young and just waiting for my next Happy Meal or tank engine. As I get older, the pain intensifies. Not only for me but also because of what my mother endured. It is as if I have two tower-shaped scars in my soul that can never heal. Every time I have a birthday, performance, or an important life event, I feel sad that my dad cannot be there. Who would have thought one morning, one telephone call would change my life forever?

This leads me to Good Grief. Now that I am fifteen, I am grateful that I can help support other children going through what I experienced—even if it is just to hand out pizza. It is all worth it. I was in their shoes once and when closing circle arrives and the children are smiling, my heart repairs itself just a little bit more.

Finding My Voice

"Good Grief also taught me to pay it forward and find ways to make the world less lonely and difficult for grieving kids."

Tyler Rivera

I want to tell you my story and why I love Good Grief. It all began when I went in for my orientation a month after my dad died. Actually, Joe, Good Grief's CEO, gave our orientation. My mother, sister, and I sat down with Joe and told him our story. My sister wasn't very pleasant about the fact that we were there. She was 17 at the time, and you know what that looks like. I'm not like that, but I was very scared to be there. It was a whole new journey for me that I could not have ever imagined would happen.

A week later we had our first group; I was 10 at the time. The group had three people, but it quickly grew to 15 because so many families needed Good Grief's help. This is how my life was at that time: I was just starting the new, scary adventures of middle school. I came to the school with no friends and didn't know anybody, and my dad's death was fresh in my memory. I was in guidance a lot of the time for the first few months of middle school. I needed a lot of help! Good Grief provided me with that help.

I was very scared to move forward. I was full of grief. I did not know how to talk about it with friends because no one understood what this experience was like for me. However, the kids at Good Grief truly understood and helped me. Hearing advice and words of encouragement from my peers made a difference; it was not like going to a guidance counselor or psychologist and being told what to do. I could trust someone who actually had the similar experience of losing a loved one! Other grieving kids taught me how to adapt, and these people became my friends. It is important that you know that we become friends at Good Grief— good friends, family friends. These friendships do not stop at Good Grief. They continue every night of the week.

My Good Grief friends have helped me support my other friends. I had a friend at school whose dad died of cancer. He did not know whether or not to go to the funeral or how to grieve. I helped him. I know that he and I are special; we have a hidden mark that other people don't understand. I told him about Good Grief, and I told him how to support his family. I was able to help others because of what Good Grief taught me. When I was in 8th grade I met a bully. A kid called me a wimp because I broke down after a teacher told me to go home and tell my mother and father that I love them. I cried because I can't say that to my dad anymore, but I knew how to get through that moment because I had my Good Grief friends. The kid made fun of me for going to so-called therapy, but now he is the one in therapy for being a bully. So ha!

Now that I am no longer at Good Grief, I miss the friends and volunteers. I miss spending time on a Tuesday night talking to people about how we are doing. Every night I learned something and had something to say. Good Grief gave me the ability to live my life. It just so happens that it gave me the ability to live my life how my father wanted me to, and that feels amazing.

Good Grief also taught me to pay it forward and find ways to make the world less lonely and difficult for grieving kids. Now, I've been telling you all about me and how important Good Grief is to me and my family, but I haven't told you about my dad.

My dad died on April 11, 2009 at 12:45pm. You might wonder why I remember those details so clearly, but I was in the room when he took his last breath. The following few days made me feel like someone was playing loud music in my ears. I was numb and tingly thinking something like this never could have happened. It felt like I was okay, but I knew I was not. I was in shock because I lost my dad who was hilarious, had an awesome personality, wore his heart on his sleeve, and didn't hurt people. I remember stories of my dad that when he was working he always donated to the women's battered shelter because he wanted to give back. He grew up in a rough area of the Bronx and understood how important giving back was. Whatever little money or time he had, he was generous and shared it with everybody. One time, we took a trip to see my aunt who has Lupus and is very sick. We went to her apartment because she had no food. We probably gave her $500 worth of food and gifts, and he did so with a smile, knowing that what he was doing was right. He did this constantly. It wasn't a one-time event. That was an important lesson for me, and I think that is why my mom and sister now volunteer at Good Grief.

As I'm looking toward the future, I want to go to college to learn audio engineering and study music. I hope to use my love of singing to teach other kids vocals. I think it is ironic that I have a dream to help people find their voice just like Good Grief helped me find mine.

A Circle of Connectedness

"There is no doubt that death is a reality we must face, ready or not. I know that all the people who have passed through the doors of Good Grief would be forced to cope with their loss even in the absence of Good Grief. But the first opening circle I witnessed some five years ago stays with me and confirms the importance and power of community."

Adam Kenney

As someone whose days left to live are most likely less than the days I have been alive, I have come to realize that there have been few, precious moments that I consider to be of real importance. These moments help define my relevance as a human: the first time I saw the Grand Canyon at dawn, the first time I held the hand of my spouse, holding my newborn sons, and witnessing the first "opening circle" at Good Grief. These are among the most important moments in my life.

The opening circle ritual at Good Grief, a time when everyone says their name and who died, is a privilege to **witness**. A circle is a good metaphor for how I think about my time at Good Grief and what I have witnessed. In that circle—almost a circle of life—children from three years old to young parents support each other as they come to understand their new realities, handed to them by death.

I imagine my Good Grief experiences like circles in a pond. They have helped me become a more centered person. Witnessing a teenager grieve and re-imagine their life has helped me try to live my life with intention—to find joy with the people I love, know, and meet on a daily basis—and to see inspiration and become awed by the human spirit. There is no doubt that death is a reality we must face, ready or not. I know that all the people who have passed through the doors of Good Grief would be forced to cope with their loss even in the absence of Good Grief. But the first Opening Circle I witnessed some five years ago stays with me and confirms the importance and power of community.

In the very first Opening Circle I witnessed, as each person introduced himself and named the person they lost, I could feel the strength of the human spirit build in the room. I could feel the vibrations of connectedness: *I am not alone; there are others that can help me and I can help them; I am not powerless; this is not what I want, but I will get through this and will be changed by my grief.* Perhaps, my Good Grief experience creates ripples in the lives of my family, friends, and acquaintances. Maybe, there is hope that through intersections of compassion and sorrow, I will better be able to come to terms with my own death.

The diversity of people I have met at Good Grief is incredible. It crosses all lines: rich, poor, religious, unreligious, young, straight, gay, traditional families, nontraditional families, estranged families, tolerant people, strongly opinionated people, and a few very prejudiced people. But death is a great equalizer. The support, hope, and inspiration I have witnessed speak to the strength that comes from diversity finding a safe place like Good Grief. Such a place allows for each person's uniqueness to interact with the commonalities of grief and healing.

Over the last years, I have had the honor of witnessing positive changes in the lives of those living with grief, one story at a time. These changes happened through tears, laughter, anger, regret, vulnerability, doubt, hope, and the entire spectrum of our human experience. It is humbling to think that this honor came to me because of my willingness to listen without judgment and simply acknowledge, "I hear you." Thank you to all the people who have allowed me to **witness** their grief journey. You give me hope and inspiration.

But I Rise

Daniel Ilkow

When life happens,
We hear cries
It is hard to overcome,
But I will rise.

So very painful,
So very hard
I mourn till this day,
But it is touching when I get a card.

I stop my sorrow,
With my red tired eyes
His memory I keep, always alive,
And that makes me rise.

I miss his food,
I loved it a lot
Now I am the chef,
I always use his pot.

He was always there,
He never lied.
Seeing his pictures,
Is the reason I rise.

Without his memory,
I know not what to do
I think of my life,
He was the glue.

Although, it is life,
And everyone eventually dies
It happened too soon,
But I rise.

He will always have,
A spot in my heart
And I will rise
Forever I will be,
Sad.

But I will rise,
I will never forget him,
His memory will forever live
I will rise
And rise
And rise.

The Invisible Tattoo

*"My children and I will always love Lance. We will never forget him. We still cry together at the most random times. We laugh at the funny things he used to do. We miss him. His headstone reads, "A Radiant Smile, A Heart of Gold," and that is the man we remember as we wear our **invisible tattoo**."*

Serpil Esbin

On December 26, 2006, our family received the life-altering news that my husband, Lance Joseph Esbin, had inoperable pancreatic cancer. The fear and horror of what was happening to us was inconceivable. How can a strong, active man with two young kids have such a dreadful disease? How can this beautiful person be facing the end of his life at the age of 36? How do we begin to wrap our brain around what was to come? That was the day we received the first marks of our *invisible* tattoo.

My name is Serpil Esbin. I am the proud mother of Seylan and Cole. My children and I bear, like so many others, the *invisible tattoo*. Loss. The loss of a loved one. A loss that is so profound that it is with you always, like a tattoo.

Not only was Lance my husband, partner, and confidant, he was also my best friend. He was the one person that allowed me to be my true self. Lance was the best father to our two children. Our daughter was five-years-old and our son was two-years-old at the time of his diagnosis. He never allowed the effects of the chemotherapy and radiation to get in the way of his time with the children. He was their number-one playmate and to this day I cannot fill his shoes, hard as I try.

Lance was born with the type of charisma that you see on a movie screen. He was the life of every party. He was very handsome yet super humble. His smile would light up a room and melt your heart. Many people said he looked like Ben Affleck or a young Mickey Rourke, but I always thought of him as Adam Sandler because he was an absolute comedian. He was extremely loyal to all of his friends and he had so many from different walks of life. His gift of gab turned many a stranger into a friend.

Ironman. Superman. These are some of the names Lance acquired during his battle with cancer. Pancreatic cancer is aggressive and most sufferers have a short battle with little quality of life. Lance received chemotherapy for four years as well as radiation. His body endured four different types of chemotherapy at the highest dosage possible. Throughout this difficult treatment, he maintained a positive attitude, always flashing that gorgeous smile.

In September 2010, we were devastated to find out that the cancer had spread. He was given a new chemotherapy treatment; the cancer laughed. At that time, I felt the markings on my *invisible* tattoo starting to fill in. I was scared, so very scared. I was sad for him, for myself and for our precious innocent children who did not deserve this. How unfair for all of us.

On November 7, 2010, we participated in the PanCan PurpleStride 5K with over 50 friends and family to raise funds to advance pancreatic cancer research, support patients, and "create hope." Lance courageously completed the entire walk and received a standing ovation from hundreds of people in attendance. For a brief moment, I thought that Lance might get lucky and beat this thing or at least just live with it. Sadly, my thoughts were just wishful thinking. One week later, he was admitted to the hospital. For the next six weeks, Memorial Sloan Kettering became my home with the exception of two unsuccessful in-home hospice attempts. On December 23, Lance was moved to Calvary Hospice in the Bronx. My ***invisible tattoo*** became darker and darker. On December 28, 2010, our beloved Lance passed away peacefully with friends and family jammed into every inch of his room.

On December 30, 2010, hundreds of people came to pay their last respects to Lance. He received six beautiful eulogies. Our beautiful and brave daughter, Seylan, gave the last eulogy. When she spoke about her father, there were no dry eyes in the chapel. At that moment, I realized that my children had lost the most.

The ceremony at the cemetery was the most difficult experience of the entire funeral service. As each person laid a white rose on the casket, my children and I held red roses. Our son, Cole, could not handle the enormity of what was happening and was taken away. Before he left, he placed his rose on the casket; the pain, confusion and anger in his eyes was unbearable. As we drove away at the end of the service, I realized that my children and I had reached the last leg of receiving our **invisible tattoo**. The ink was dry.

Grief. We have loss, so we grieve. Yet, there are no rules to grieving. So how does a parent who is wrapped up in grief make sure that their child is properly grieving? Well, I read books and did research online. However, I fell short because I did not have a handle on my own feelings. I needed my children to feel normal and not so isolated since none of their friends or classmates had lost a parent to death (many children "lose" a parent due to divorce, military service, etc.). During my research, I stumbled across Good Grief. My children finally connected with other children who are in the same situation, experiencing loss. Every person we met had the **invisible tattoo**, loss. We felt a sense of community and deeper understanding of our own experience.

My children and I will always love Lance. We will never forget him. We still cry together at the most random times. We laugh at the funny things he used to do. We miss him. His headstone reads, "A Radiant Smile, A Heart of Gold," and that is the man we remember as we wear our **invisible tattoo**.

Made in the USA
Lexington, KY
16 December 2014